LIVE
LABOR
LOVE

The History
of a
Northern Family
1700-1900

Alene Smith
Adeline Tucker

Alene Jackson Smith
and
Adeline Jackson Tucker

HERITAGE BOOKS
2007

HERITAGE BOOKS

AN IMPRINT OF HERITAGE BOOKS, INC.

Books, CDs, and more—Worldwide

For our listing of thousands of titles see our website
at
www.HeritageBooks.com

Published 2007 by
HERITAGE BOOKS, INC.
Publishing Division
65 East Main Street
Westminster, Maryland 21157-5026

International Standard Book Number: 978-0-7884-3176-0

To Our Father and Mother

Blyden and Gertrude Jackson

Acknowledgements

We are indebted to many persons for their assistance in making this book possible.

To Hunter College of the City University of New York for the Schuster Grant Award to pursue the research for this book.

To the members of the Jean Sampson Scott Greater New York Chapter of the African American Historical and Genealogical Society: Doris Burbridge, Richard Burbridge, Augustus Harris, Cheryl McDaniels, Andrea Ramsey and Sandra Redman for their feedback, editorial comments and support throughout the writing of this book.

To Adelaide Marek, Town Historian in Brookfield, Connecticut, for her interest and perseverance in researching the life of Robin Starr, Revolutionary War figure. Her willingness to share her research was most appreciated.

To Lorraine Roberts, President of the African American Chapter of the Dutchess County Historical Society for her continued interest and encouragement.

To the Dutchess County Historical Society and the Litchfield County Historical Society for providing a forum for us to present our research.

To Edna Baker Carnegie, long time New Haven resident, for her oral history that led us to great finds.

To extended family: Ward Potter, Lewis Jackson, Carter Rowe and George Jackson for the oral histories, pictures and information that augmented our research.

To Marion Sachdeva, Julio Hernandez Delgado and Sally Milgrim for their continued support and for reading the manuscript.

To Adeline's children, Renee and Karen and to Alene's children George Jr. and Beth for their enthusiasm and interest in this book. They are the next generation.

To Alene's husband George Sr., for his support and constant reading of the manuscript.

CONTENTS

Preface

Ancestral Home

As young children, our mother, Gertrude Lohman Jackson, had two bits of genealogical information that she shared with us about our paternal ancestors. We often smiled because Mother knew more about our father, Blyden Jackson's family, than he did. She was the repository of family wit, wisdom and history. She mentioned that our paternal Great Grandfather, known only as Rowe, was a missionary to Africa. We did not know Rowe and had never heard talk of him or seen his picture. This was heady stuff about Africa, and it conjured up exotic pictures in our minds as we envisioned our great grandfather, with a missionary zeal, going off to a far away land to preach the Gospel.

The other piece of information was that our paternal grandmother, Agnes Adeline Rowe Jackson, Rowe's daughter, was born in Litchfield, Connecticut. As children growing up in New Haven, Connecticut, we visited her and we remember vividly her rather neat appearance and meticulous dress. Even when she was in her late seventies and she walked with a cane, she always had on a dark dress with a lace collar, and was very prim and proper. She was once a school teacher and pillar of St. Luke's Episcopal Church in New Haven, Connecticut. That was where her children and her children's children went to Sunday School. "Ma," as we called her, was a small woman about five feet tall, very fair with long straight hair.

It was not until we began our genealogical research some years later that we discovered who this Rowe really was and the extent to which our paternal family were longtime northerners. In our genealogical pilgrimage, we traced our paternal lineage back six generations, in the North, to the 1740s. Our family: the Rowes, Jacksons and Fowlers claim Litchfield County in northwest Connecticut and Dutchess County in northeast New

1

York as their ancestral homeland. Along with our relatives, there was a small black presence in both these counties. Dating back to the 1700s, African Americans resided in the many small towns where we are doing our research. Towns such as Canaan, Cornwall, Goshen, Kent, Litchfield, Salisbury and Sharon in Litchfield, County and towns such as Amenia, Pine Plains, Smithfield, Stanford and Washington in Dutchess, County. The roots of our ancestors, as well as many other African Americans, are buried deep in this northern land and it is this soil that has nurtured them for all these many generations.

Introduction

Litchfield County in Connecticut and Dutchess County in New York border one another. They are counties settled among the rolling hills of the Berkshire Mountains. In the 1600s before these two counties were established, Native Americans inhabited the area. There was often fighting among the various nations, and the area between the two counties was a no-man's land. Tribes dared not venture here for fear of loss of life. The area now called Litchfield was known to the Indians as Bantam. The western part of Litchfield was considered a wasteland. The Native Americans who inhabited it came from many different tribal nations in upstate New York, Massachusetts, and other parts of Connecticut and Canada.

When the Puritans came to Connecticut from Massachusetts, they first settled in Hartford, Windsor and Wethersfield located in the eastern part of Connecticut. About the 1720s they began to move into the western section. Confrontations with the Native Americans ensued and eventually the Indians were almost decimated. By the late 1700s, few Native Americans remained. Most were remnants of a variety of nations. Extensive travel by the White settlers began to take place from Boston, Massachusetts to Hartford, Connecticut to Litchfield, Connecticut and into Dutchess County in eastern New York. Roads that were once Indian trails were blazed for commercial and military purposes. Later, these roads became highways between New York and Connecticut. The English were the predominant group that settled in Litchfield County, and the Dutch were the largest group that settled in Dutchess County.

During the 1700s, Blacks in colonial New England and New York were a mixture of slaves and freemen. Many of the large seaport towns such as Hartford, New London and Fairfield located in the eastern part of Connecticut were ports where slave trading and commerce took place. This resulted in a large population of slaves. In comparison, Litchfield County, located inland in the northwest corner of the state, had a relatively smaller Black population and fewer slaves. Many of these slaves

3

came from the West Indies, particularly Barbados. Piersen (1988)[1] gives figures on the Negro population of Connecticut from 1756-1790. A comparison of two of the counties will give the reader an idea of the differences among the counties.

County	1756	1774	1782a	1790a
New London	829	1194	1920	1315
Litchfield	54	331	529	556

a: Includes Indians

The topography in Litchfield made it difficult to do large farming and what crops were grown did not require great numbers of laborers. Hence, there were fewer slaves. By the same token, Dutchess County had two different types of land areas. The three largest towns, Fishkill, Rhinebeck, and Poughkeepsie, located in the Hudson Valley along the Hudson River, had large farms and hence a greater need for slaves to do manual labor and to farm. The remaining towns, however, such as Amenia and Pine Plains, located in the northern part of the county, did not have as many slaves because the farms were smaller and they were not located along a river. The early African arrivals were a mixture of indentured servants, slaves and freemen. Some of them became skilled workers in a variety of jobs such as wagoners, shoemakers, barbers and even a few medical specialists who had learned their trade by working with a doctor. These craftsmen were very much a presence in early colonial life. Some northern slaves lived in the house of the master and sat and ate with their owners. Because of the close proximity of slave and master, they were often treated as members of the family. Regardless, slavery was still a deplorable state of being not having your freedom.

Slaves had no political rights and were subjected to strict laws called the "Black Codes." These laws required Blacks to carry passes when they traveled. They could not buy alcoholic beverages, sell goods to Whites, argue with or strike a White person or be out after 9:00 p.m.

Free Blacks who arrived here as indentured servants for

4

White families from England were often included in the codes. They would have to carry passes when traveling outside of their own limits. They could not socialize with the slaves or serve on juries. They were taxed like the Whites, but they could not hold office. Not all Whites agreed with the Black Codes or with slavery. In 1774, many colonists were beginning to speak out against slavery and also beginning to protest the refusal of the Colonies to enlist Blacks in the militia.

According to Lorenzo Greene (1969),[2] the distribution of Negroes in Connecticut in 1774, in those towns where our ancestors resided, was as follows:

Town	Whites	Blacks
Cornwall	957	17
Goshen	1,098	13
Kent	1,922	74
Litchfield	2,509	45
Salisbury	1,936	44
Sharon	1,986	26

Life in Black Colonial New England and New York was difficult. Often there were fewer African women. African males therefore frequently married Native Americans or White women. At this time, there were no laws against intermarriage. Hence, our own ancestors are a tri-racial group - African, Native American and White. They were slaves and free.

The church was a very important part of life in early America. The Congregational Church was organized in Connecticut in the early 1630s by the English Puritans from the Massachusetts Bay Colony. In 1721, the first Congregational Church in Litchfield was formed. This denomination was the one to which many of our ancestors belonged and its records provided important information about some of our relatives. It also helped build the spiritual foundation for our ancestors and one relative was ordained as a minister of the Gospel in this denomination.

During the American Revolutionary War, in which the Colonists were fighting for their freedom, Africans joined the struggle because they thought they would also be free. At first, Africans were not welcomed into the Continental Army. When the need for additional men became great, they were pressed into service. Often, they took the place of a White person, either their master or employer. We have identified one African, Robin Starr, from Sharon, Connecticut who played a role in this most significant of wars. While he is not an ancestor, we want to lift his life up as being representative of the African presence in the War. It was after the Revolutionary War that religious groups, particularly the Quakers, and Abolitionist Societies, began to fight to abolish slavery. While this struggle met with less resistance in Connecticut, the Dutch in New York steadfastly resisted any attempts to abolish slavery. They saw the slaves as extremely important to their economic existence.

Connecticut in 1784 passed the Gradual Emancipation Act. Manumitted slaves born after March 1, 1784 had to serve as indentured servants until they reached age 25. Slaves who fought in the American Revolution were freed after their service. In New York, it was not until 1799 that a Gradual Emancipation Act was passed. This law allowed all Negro Children to be free after maturity. This meant age 28 for men and 25 for women. In 1817, Manumission was set at age 21 in New York.

The period from 1800-1860 was a less restrictive time for Blacks in the North. They were involved in the Abolitionist Movement along with Whites of good will. They were aware of the plight of their southern brethren. Our relatives were part of this struggle. Indeed one relative, George Clinton Rowe, eventually went south to preach and teach. The first Black National Negro Convention, which took place in Syracuse, New York in October 1864, had 144 delegates from 18 states. Blacks wanted the right to vote. However, in New York if you had $250.00 dollars worth of property, you were eligible to vote.

In 1861, the American Civil War began. Blacks, though willing to fight, at first were not allowed to serve. They eventually were enlisted and made a significant contribution from the well heralded 54th Massachusetts Colored Regiment to the 29th Connecticut Colored Regiment where several members of our family were enrolled. In any case, African Americans have fought in the Revolutionary War, the War of 1812, the Civil War and all the other wars in which our country called its citizens to take up arms.

This was the background that influenced northern African Americans from the 18th century to today. They had hopes and dreams that one day they would be accepted as first class citizens in the only country they knew and loved. They longed to fulfill their destinies here in beautiful Connecticut and New York. The story of our ancestors is but one example of the Black presence in the North during these times. This history is written so that historical substance is given to the role Blacks played in the development and life of our country.

Quarles (1987) states, "Except for the first settlers at Jamestown, the Negro's roots in the original thirteen colonies sink deeper than any other group from across the Atlantic. Afro-Americans helped to make America what it was and what it is."[3] The history of the Jackson family, like many other African Americans, is an example of those whose lives are threads interwoven into the history of this country.

Chapter One

The Starrs of Sharon, Connecticut

Our genealogical pilgrimage brought us to Sharon, Connecticut, a lovely old New England town in the northwest corner of Litchfield County. It was settled in the 1700s. The town is surrounded by a number of large placid ponds. Two of its most notable are Lake Silver (Mudge Pond) and Weequaghock (Indian Pond). Old tree-lined roadways and rolling hills create a magnificent landscape. In the very early years, the southeastern part of Sharon, which runs along the majestic Housatonic River and junctions at Cornwall Bridge, was known as Ellsworth, Connecticut. In later years it would become part of Sharon proper. It was in Ellsworth that the Starrs, an African American family, lived, owned property, tilled the soil, paid taxes, fought in the military and died.

Oral history told us that our 2nd Gt Grandmother was Adeline Agnes Starr from Sharon. For many years, as we did our research, we gathered information on the Starrs. In fact several legal documents list Adeline as a Starr. We would learn later that Adeline was really named Adeline Agnes Starr Ferguson from Goshen, Connecticut. Is there a connection to the Starrs of Sharon? This we have not been able to establish. Although we do not know if there is a direct link between Adeline and the Starrs, we claim the Starrs as spiritual kindred. We lift up their story.

The 1790 Census of Connecticut[1] lists a Robin Starr, free Black head of household with a wife, and one child. (In later documents he changed his name to Robert. For what purpose? We do not know). Where did they come from? What was life like for them? What did they look like? According to Good enough (1890),[2] Robin Starr was brought to Danbury, Connecticut from Guinea, West Africa. He was a slave of Josiah Starr, a Captain in the Army who resided in Danbury, Connecticut with his family in the late 1600s.

Many are not aware that the North held slaves just like the

South. While there were some large plantations, in many areas slaves were few in number and hence were often treated as servants and sometimes even ate at the same table as their owners. "Black Codes," however, used to restrict the movement and regulate the lives of slaves, often subjected them to dehumanizing conditions and served to remind them that they were not free. It was ironic that at this moment in the history and life of the colonies, Blacks were living in legal bondage while the colonists were about to fight for freedom from English domination.

The political atmosphere in the colonies was in an upheaval. In the late 1700s, the relationship with England was under a strain because of the Seven Years War between England and France. The English were in need of revenue, so they began to tax the Colonists. Through a series of Parliamentary Acts from England, such as the Sugar Act and the Stamp Act, England was able to obtain revenue from them by requiring them to use a special stamped paper from London for all legal purposes. The Colonists were becoming irritated with England about these taxes and felt they were being taxed without representation. As relations with England worsened, the incident known as the Boston Tea Party precipitated the American Revolution, which took place from 1775-1783.

The Colonists called together the Continental Army headed by General George Washington. There was much debate about Blacks, free or slave, joining the army. Blacks were very willing and anxious to join. They were not only ready to fight for the liberty of the colonies but wanted to fight for the freedom of all Blacks as well.

Robin Starr's pension record[3] states that he entered the Continental Army in 1777 and fought until 1783, the duration of the war. He fought in the 2nd Company, 2nd Regiment under Colonel Herman Swift. This was an integrated unit comprised of free Blacks, slaves, and Whites who fought side by side. On his pension application he states that he fought in seven battles: Lake Champlain, NY; Danbury, CT; Germantown, PA;

Monmouth, NY; Norwalk, CT; Stony Point, NY; and the Battle of Yorktown in VA. Robin was wounded in the first and last battles.

In 1783, there was a reorganization of regiments and Robin was transferred to the 2nd Company, 4th Regiment which had all Black soldiers. He was 26 years old when he joined and was discharged at the age of 32. Upon his discharge, he received the Badge of Merit which was created by General Washington and given to non-commissioned soldiers who showed bravery, fidelity and good conduct.[4] In addition, Robin received a Certificate of Discharge signed by General Washington, acknowledging his service in the Revolutionary War. We are sure he stood tall in his uniform as he received the Badge of Merit for six years of faithful service from Colonel H. Swift of the 2nd Connecticut Regiment. Robin's name appears in the following books: *Minority Military Service Connecticut 1775-1783*[5] and *Connecticut's Black Soldiers 1775-1783*[6]

In 1781, while still in the service, Robin bought his freedom and that of a woman called Chole for 40 pounds. We are not sure who Chole was but we wonder if it could have been his mother, because often freed slaves bought their mother's freedom, or could it have been his wife whose name was later changed to Lilly? It is interesting that Robin had changed his own name to Robert.

Many slaves who served in the Revolutionary War received a tract of land. What is interesting in the case of Robin is that he received his freedom for fighting and yet paid 40 pounds for his freedom, and his tract of land went to an officer named Isaac Trowbridge. We have not located any particulars regarding this transaction. After the war, Robin settled in Ellsworth, Connecticut in a section called Guinea. We assume it was called this because many of its residents were free Blacks from Guinea, West Africa.

The Federal government set up the pension system for War veterans on July 4, 1820. At the age of 69, Robin Starr applied for his pension which he received on October 19, 1820. In his pension records, he said, "I am crippled so that I cannot walk without my crutches. My left thigh has been broken and I have not been able to labor for the past ten years."[7] We do not know if these medical problems were the result of action in the war, hard work during slavery, or old age.

At the time of his application his property consisted of:

1 large iron kettle	$1.00
5 old chairs	.84
1 great chair	.50
A little crockery	$2.00
2 tables	$3.00
1 six qt. pot	.50
Total	$7.84

His
Robin   X   Starr
Mark

The X used in his name indicated that Robin could not write his name.

The Probate Court Records from Sharon, Connecticut[8] indicate that Robert and Lilly later owned some property in Sharon. Over the years, the property was sold and the last tract of land, which they lived on, was bequeathed to their son Abel. Robert Starr died in April 1832 and Lilly died sometime between 1829 and 1830. They both died in Sharon, Connecticut but their burial sites are unknown.

After the death of Robin, his son, Abel applied for his pension. When we saw Robin's original pension papers in the National Archives in Washington, D.C. the pension did not indicate his son's name. Thus we were unable to make the link between Abel and Robin. As fate would have it, in February 2000, we met Adelaide Marek, Town Historian for Brookfield, Connecticut which is part of Danbury, Connecticut. She had been researching the life of Robin Starr for twenty years. Her

11

interest in him began while researching Danbury history for the Nation's Bicentennial in 1976. She gave us a piece of research from the Hartford County Records of 1883[9] that proved Abel was indeed the son of Robin. We were elated to make the connection. We are indebted to Ms. Marek for her interest and perseverance in researching Robin Starr. We felt an emotional sense of pride as we read the historical accomplishments of Robert and Lilly Starr.

Robin and Lilly's son, Abel, was born in 1791 in Sharon, Connecticut. He either worked the land, or did some kind of labor at the forge or mill in the area. On November 2, 1820 he married Betsy Weston of Stratford, Connecticut. Van Alstyne (1897),[10] records the marriage. Abel and Betsy eventually lived on the land passed down to them from his parents, Robert and Lilly.

Abel and Betsy were farmers and like most farmers probably rose early to farm, fix carriages, mend the belts and saddles, sew and cook. At times, Abel hired himself out to neighboring farms to earn additional money. The farmers grew potatoes, corn, tomatoes, barley and raised cows and horses. There were also barns to be mended. The Starrs attended the local Congregational Church on Sunday mornings. We can imagine the family sitting around the table having a big Sunday breakfast and then getting their children, Caroline, Josiah and Lewis, ready for Church. The women wore long dresses and colorful bonnets while the men wore their best Sunday-go-to-meeting pants and suspenders. During the week, when Betsy was not cooking or mending, she probably spent time teaching the children.

Abel and Betsy lived in a transitional time. The country was again experiencing problems with England and in December 1807, Congress passed the Embargo Act. This act stopped all trade with England and made it illegal for any American vessel to leave an American port. New Haven, New London, Norwich, Milford and Hartford were famous Connecticut seaports which were affected by the embargo. Exports such as wood, cotton, and silk were threatened. The British were capturing American ships. The Starrs, like many others, were affected by a shortage of jobs. There was tension and much discussion about fighting in another war. But on June 18, 1812, the United States declared war on Great Britain. Records at the Connecticut State Library in Hartford along with a book by Goodenough (1890),[11] indicate that when the call to arms came, Abel Starr, along with other Black patriots, heeded the call and fought in the War of 1812. Starr (1926)[12] lists Abel Starr's death as March 6, 1881 at the age of 90-"flag." The notation flag denotes a soldier's grave. Abel is buried in the soldiers' plot in Calhoun Cemetery in Cornwall, Connecticut.[13] We do not know where Betsey is buried.

We can glimpse a bit about the life of the Starrs through Abel's will.[14] He left five dollars to his daughter Caroline, who was married, five dollars to his son Lewis, and Josiah received all 37 acres of land. The reason given for this is the fact that Josiah financially helped and took care of Abel for a long period of time.

Again in 1860 the United States was experiencing problems but this time it was the eve of the Civil War. Frederick Douglass lobbied for the use of Black troops in combat. It is said, "Frederick Douglass was the conscience of the nation." He argued the war was not just for bringing the nation together, but to end slavery, bring equality to Black folks and make them a part of American society. President Abraham Lincoln was sworn in as president of the Union on March 4, 1861. His middle of the road stand on slavery did not satisfy the North or the South. But he promised to carry out the laws of the Union and to protect all properties of the government. On April 13, 1861, the first shots were fired at Fort Sumter in Charleston Harbor, South Carolina. When Major Anderson refused to give up the fort, the authorities in Charleston claimed this was an act of war. This series of events was followed by the South seceding from the Union. South Carolina seceded first on December 20, 1861, followed by Mississippi January 9th, Florida January 10th, Alabama January 11, Georgia January 19th,

Louisiana January 26th and Texas February 1st. Representatives from the seceded states met in Alabama and organized a provisional government. Jefferson Davis was chosen president of the confederate states. Later, Virginia, Arkansas, North Carolina and Tennessee seceded. President Lincoln issued a call to arms. Blacks as always were ready to serve their country. But the national debate whether Blacks should be allowed to fight raged on. Frederick Douglass and the Abolitionist Movement had a profound effect on the outcome, and in 1863 a number of Black Regiments were formed.

The Starr boys were mustered to fight in the Civil War. Josiah Starr was a sergeant and Lewis Starr, was a corporal. They fought in the Twenty-Ninth Colored Regiment Infantry, Company C. They joined from Sharon, Connecticut, but they enlisted in Danbury, Connecticut and embarked from Fair Haven, Connecticut. According to an article by Reverend Henry G. Marshall (1889),[15] the Captain of Company I, Twenty- Ninth Connecticut Volunteers, Colonel Wooster was in command and the Regiment saw action. The 29th left for Annapolis, Maryland and then Hilton Head, South Carolina, where it remained for four months. On August 8th, the 29th sailed for Bermuda Hundred, Virginia. At this point, they were incorporated into an all Black Brigade in an all Black Division. This Division, along with the Eighteenth Corps, helped to take Fort Harrison, just outside of Richmond, Virginia. The troops then fought at Darby Town Road, along with the Army of the Potomac, where they drove the enemy into the woods and kept them there.

During the Battle of Chafins Town, Kell House, Virginia on October 27, 1864, Josiah was wounded through the left cheekbone by a musket ball. He later returned to the fighting. This all Black Division received special commendation for bravery and gallantry in action at Chafins Farm and Darby Town Road near Richmond, Virginia. The 29th was the first Infantry Unit to enter Richmond, the Confederate Capital, which fell in April 1865.

Josiah was mustered out on October 24th 1865. Lewis also fought valiantly, was promoted to Corporal on July 15, 1864 and

14

was discharged on May 16, 1865. Josiah Starr is buried in Calhoun Cemetery in Cornwall, Connecticut along with his father, Abel. How fitting, since he was the son who cared for his father for so many years and was remembered by his father in his will. Lewis is buried in Spring Drive Cemetery in Darien, Connecticut.

The New Haven, Connecticut descendants of the 29th have shared some of their research with us. Among these writings is a piece by J .J. Hill, who had been a member of the 29th. The author, Hill (1867),[16] learned to read and write and later became a minister and joined the 29th Connecticut Regiment on January 7, 1864. His sketch is a powerful story of the battles the men of the 29th fought. We also feel a kinship with the Starrs because several of our relatives fought in the 29th Regiment also.

After the Civil War, the northern soldiers formed the Grand Army of the Republic. This Veterans Association was represented in almost every town throughout the United States. In 1868, General John A. Logan, Commander-in-Chief of the Republic, announced that May 30th would be known as Memorial Day. It is now a national holiday honoring the memory of all who served in wars for the United States. Two hundred thousand blacks fought in the Union Army and one in every four men in the Union Navy was a Black. Surely these Blacks, as well as the Starrs, deserve to be honored for their services. At the war's end in 1865, the black troops were never allowed to march in triumph down Pennsylvania Avenue with the White troops. This is why we felt proud when we attended the 1998 dedication of the Black Civil War Monument in Washington, D.C. which honors the Black soldiers who fought in the Civil War. The dedication of the monument gave their descendants a chance to march for them. A sense of excitement was in the air that day in Washington as preparations for the march began. Those men who would reenact the Civil War events were dressed in the blue uniforms of the Union Army and they were lined up on the street going through their drills. Some of the women were dressed in long skirts and carried parasols indicative of the Civil War Period. Descendants of the soldiers were mingling and greeting one another as they moved to be with their respective state units. We marched with the Connecticut 29th Colored Regiment. A profound sense of the historical moment and the feeling of oneness pervaded the participants. Then the ruffle of drums brought us to attention. The soldiers moved forward and we fell in behind them. What a glorious feeling as we marched down Pennsylvania Avenue. We were not marching for ourselves but for all our ancestors and all those early patriots who had fought and given their lives for freedom. Finally they would receive the recognition they deserved. As we marched into the area of the statue, a hush moved across the crowd. The dedication of the monument was a very moving and solemn moment. Many had tears in their eyes as the statue was unveiled and dedicated posthumously to all the Black Patriots. We stood in awe as they played taps. We knew their time had finally come.

The Starr Family has earned a place in the military history of this country. They fought as patriots in all the early wars. They were representative of the northern African Americans and the contribution they made to this country. African Americans would continue to defend this country in all the subsequent wars.

Yes! This is Our Fathers' Land.

Ancestors of Alene and Adeline Jackson

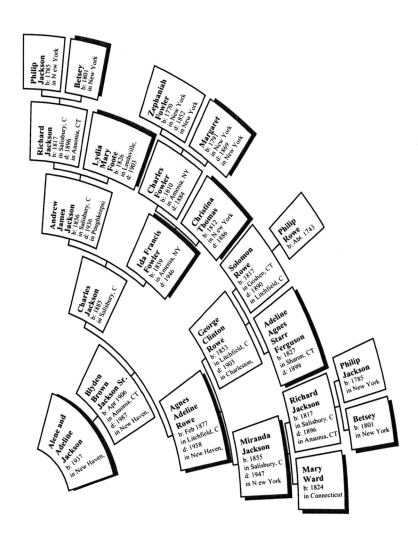

Philip Jackson b: 1785 in New York

Betsey b: 1801 in New York

Richard Jackson b: 1817 in Salisbury, C d: 1896 in Ansonia, CT

Lydia Mary Foote b: 1826 in Leedsville,

Zephaniah Fowler b: 1770 in New York d: 1852 in New York

Margaret b: 1791 in New York d: 1869 in New York

Andrew James Jackson b: 1856 in Salisbury, C d: 1936 in Poughkeepsi

Charles Fowler b: 1810 in Amenia, NY d: 1884

Christina Thomas b: 1812 in New York d: 1886

Philip Rowe b: Abt. 1743

Charles Jackson b: 1885 in Salisbury, C

Ida Francis Fowler b: 1859 in Amenia, NY d: 1946

Solomon Rowe b: 1817 in Goshen, CT d: 1890 in Litchfield, C

George Clinton Rowe b: 1853 in Litchfield, C d: 1903 in Charleston.

Adeline Agnes Starr Ferguson b: 1827 in Sharon, CT d: 1899

Philip Jackson b: 1785 in New York

Blyden Brown Jackson Sr. b: Apr 1906 in Ansonia, CT d: 1987 in New Haven.

Agnes Adeline Rowe b: Feb 1877 in Litchfield, C d: 1958 in New Haven,

Richard Jackson b: 1817 in Salisbury, C d: 1896 in Ansonia, CT

Betsey b: 1801 in New York

Alene and Adeline Jackson b: 1937 in New Haven.

Miranda Jackson b: 1855 in Salisbury, C d: 1947 in New York

Mary Ward b: 1824 in Connecticut

17

Chapter Two

The Jacksons of Salisbury, Connecticut

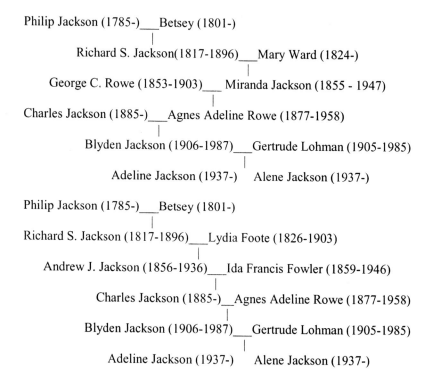

Philip Jackson (1785-)___Betsey (1801-)
|
Richard S. Jackson(1817-1896)___Mary Ward (1824-)
|
George C. Rowe (1853-1903)___ Miranda Jackson (1855 - 1947)
|
Charles Jackson (1885-)___Agnes Adeline Rowe (1877-1958)
|
Blyden Jackson (1906-1987)___Gertrude Lohman (1905-1985)
|
Adeline Jackson (1937-)   Alene Jackson (1937-)

Philip Jackson (1785-)___Betsey (1801-)
|
Richard S. Jackson (1817-1896)___Lydia Foote (1826-1903)
|
Andrew J. Jackson (1856-1936)___Ida Francis Fowler (1859-1946)
|
Charles Jackson (1885-)__Agnes Adeline Rowe (1877-1958)
|
Blyden Jackson (1906-1987)___Gertrude Lohman (1905-1985)
|
Adeline Jackson (1937-)   Alene Jackson (1937-)

Note: For purposes of this book only the names mentioned in the Jackson chapter appear on the genealogy chart.

As children, we, the authors, spent a summer at an Episcopal Church Camp in Canaan, Connecticut. It is located in the northwest corner of the state. As we traveled there, we passed the famous 19th century Cornwall Covered Bridge, one of the oldest covered bridges in America. A fond memory of that summer was the climb up Canaan Mountain, the tallest peak in Canaan. Little did we know in the 1950s that just south of Canaan are the towns of Salisbury, Cornwall, Goshen, Kent and

Litchfield where our ancestors the Jacksons lived for many generations. Perhaps they too had roamed this area and climbed this peak. The Jacksons represent another aspect of the northern African American experience.

The Jacksons were of mixed ancestry. While oral history tells us that our people have Native American roots, it has been difficult establishing which Nation. The information we have is circumstantial. A family acquaintance in New Haven, Edna Baker Carnegie, told us she remembers that the tribe the Jacksons belonged to began with a P. Could it be the Potatuck, Paquannock, Paugussett or Pequot? We also heard that our people were Iroquois and Blackfoot. Edna's sister, Constance Baker Motley, writes in her book *Equal Justice Under Law*[1] that she remembers our Great Grandmother, Miranda Jackson Rowe, was a Native American, who visited her daughter each summer in New Haven. Miranda's residence was in Kent, Connecticut.

Native Americans had been in Connecticut for centuries. As the Europeans moved into western Connecticut in the 1700s, they displaced the Native Americans. Wars, sickness and unfortunate land deals decimated the Native population. As their lands were taken, they reached the poverty level. In 1740, the Moravians, a religious group, who were originally located in the Shekomeko Indian Village, which today is Pine Plains, New York, moved to Kent, Connecticut. It was their work among the Native peoples that helped the tribes to survive. A church was built and a congregation established among the Native Americans[2].

A Schaghticoke tribal group was established there by Gideon Mauwehu, a Pequot. Mauwehu, on a hunting expedition, discovered the beautiful Housatonic Valley with a great river running through it bordered by magnificent mountains. He then decided to make this a camping ground for his people. This was a haven for the remnants of many tribal groups that had existed in large numbers in Western Connecticut and even parts of New York. The Schaghticoke group was composed of the Potatucks,

19

Pequots, and New Milford according to Atwater (1897).[3]

Over the years, some of the Native Peoples intermarried with Whites and Blacks, some relinquished their Indian identity and became taxpaying citizens and others moved on to Wisconsin, New York, Massachusetts, Canada and other locales.

Present day Schaghticoke state that the original tribe was made up primarily of Weantinock Indians from New Milford, Connecticut. Some Mahican Indians from northwest Connecticut and from neighboring New York joined the group later.

The Schaghticoke Tribal Nation exists today in Connecticut. They have gained federal recognition and plan to open a casino in Connecticut.

The Native peoples in this area had historically followed traditional patterns of seasonal movement along the Housatonic River. They fished for bass, and trout, and they hunted in the vast wooded areas. They wove beautiful baskets representative of a culture and people. They decorated them with the natural dyes available, including the purple red berries of the pokeweed. Later, they joined Blacks and Whites in farming wheat or working in the dairies.

The Litchfield area was famous for its iron ore. Beginning in the late 1700s, there were mines in Salisbury, Kent and other surrounding villages. The first blast furnace was built in Salisbury, Connecticut. Laborers cast mortars, cannons and other supplies for the Revolutionary War. Later they wrought nails, wagon tires and utensils. Iron making was one of the most important industries of the Housatonic Valley. We feel that many of our relatives might have been employed in these areas. The railroad was being built in the early 1800s, and that was another source of employment in Litchfield County. Salisbury was also an agricultural town. Wheat was the largest crop, and barley and flax were also grown.

The farthest we have been able to trace back in the Jackson line is to Philip Jackson, our 3rd Gt Grandfather, born in 1785 in New York. His wife, Betsey, was also born there. We first find them in the censuses of 1830 and 1840 in Connecticut.[4] They had to have come to Salisbury, Connecticut at least by 1817 because the census of 1850[4] indicates their children were born there.

One of the offspring of Philip and Betsey Jackson was their son, Richard, our 2nd Gt Grandfather who was born in 1817 in Salisbury, Connecticut. We had discovered Richard in our search and for five years we had a census sheet with the names Philip Jackson and Richard Jackson listed one under the other. We did not know who this Philip was until we made a discovery while researching in Ansonia, Connecticut. Eureka! We found Richard's death certificate and we discovered that Philip Jackson was his father[5]. They resided next door to one another. It is interesting to note that when Richard was age 32 and his wife was 26, they were just starting their young family. Meanwhile, his father, Philip at age 65 and his wife at age 49 still had young children. Families were large in those days and this was common.

Interestingly, the 1830 and 1840 censuses from Salisbury, Connecticut indicate that Philip and Betsey were White[6]. In the 1850 Census[7], Philip and Betsey, as well as Richard and Mary, are listed as Mulatto. By 1860[8] Philip and Betsey are not listed. Richard and Mary are listed as Mulatto. By 1870[9], Richard and Mary are listed as Black. In some cases, after the Civil War, the government designated all persons of color including Indians, as Black.

We believe that some of the extended Jackson family fought in the Civil War. Samuel Jackson was in the Connecticut 7th Regiment and Edward Jackson was in Co. E. of the 29th Colored

Regiment from Litchfield, Connecticut.

Richard grew up in Salisbury. He was a farmer and day laborer. He married Mary Ward, also from Salisbury. He and his wife had at least 12 children. As was true of large early American families, the children probably had some schooling, but they were expected to work and help the family. Some of the children lived on neighboring farms and did farm work. In the case of the females, they often did domestic work for others. In 1857, Richard and Mary had a set of twins named Miranda and Amanda. Miranda is our 2nd Gt Grandmother.

In 1874, Miranda married George Clinton Rowe from Litchfield,[10] whom we will discuss in more detail in the chapter on the Rowes. In 1876, Amanda, her twin, married Robert Linason also from Connecticut.[11] They all resided in Litchfield. Several years later, Miranda would leave Connecticut and travel South with her husband.

We had heard about Miranda being a twin through oral history, but now we established it through records and learned for the first time the name of Miranda's twin sister. We were fascinated to come across twins because we, the authors, are identical twins. We had met Miranda once when we were about ten years old. Our parents took us to New York City where Miranda was living with her daughter, Wilhelmina Rowe Carter.

Our memories are clouded because it was many years ago. It was all a bit frightening to have to tiptoe into a darkened room to see this elderly bedridden woman who did not really recognize who we were. We remember her as being fair skinned with long straight white hair framing her face. We were not able to appreciate who she was at the time. Miranda was referred to as Mama Rowe. She must have ruled with an iron fist because the story goes that you did not cross Mama Rowe. She was strict and meant business and said something only once. Pictures of her show a woman who is tall and stately. She had a

22

commanding presence.

Miranda Jackson Rowe's death certificate provided us with an interesting piece of information. It listed her father with his Indian name: Richard "Koonk a Pot" Jackson[12]. It is fascinating that there was a Sachem or Chief of the Mohican Tribe called Chief Konkapot. The Konkapots were a well known Native American family. This could be a lead for us in our search. Miranda died in New York City in 1947 and is buried in Litchfield, Connecticut.

By the late 1800s some of the Jacksons had migrated to Ansonia, Connecticut, a small town just outside of New Haven. About 1884, Richard and his wife, Mary, moved there to reside with some of their children. Richard spent his last years working as a coachman. He died in 1896 and is buried in the Pine Grove Cemetery in Ansonia, Connecticut. His wife of many years is also buried there, but we have no dates for her. It is fascinating how families gravitate to one another. Richard and his wife were there as well as their daughter, Amanda. Miranda returned to Ansonia after the death of her husband, George Rowe in 1903. She had spent 24 years working beside her husband in the South as he pastored a variety of churches. She returned to her native land for solace and to mourn her loss. She found comfort in being back with her father and sister and her people. Indeed, she eventually resided in Kent, Connecticut where the Schaghticoke Nation was located.

Agnes Adeline, our Grandmother, who was born in Litchfield but left at age two to go South with her parents, Miranda and George Rowe, also returned to Ansonia in the early 1900s. She was educated in the South and we believe she might have attended Avery Institute, an American Missionary Association Institution in Charleston, South Carolina. We also believe she stayed on to teach in South Carolina after graduation. We were told that she was once a teacher. She and her family were very much a part of the black social life of Charleston in the late

1800s. Her father was a prominent preacher and teacher as well as editor of the Charleston Enquirer. Agnes Adeline eventually married a man named Snipes who was an undertaker, or so the oral history goes. The marriage did not last, and Adeline returned to Ansonia also. She had been in the South for about twenty- four years. It must have been culture shock to return from the culturally sophisticated Charleston to a small rural town like Ansonia. Several years later Adeline would marry a second time to a man named Charles Jackson, who is our grandfather. Charles was from Salisbury.

According to vital records, our Great Grandmother, Miranda Jackson Rowe's father is Richard Jackson and her mother is Mary Ward. Our Great Grandfather, Andrew Jackson's parents are Richard Jackson and Lydia Foote.
Miranda and Andrew have the same father. If this is so, it would make their children Agnes Adeline and Charles first cousins. If you check the chart at the beginning of the chapter, you will see that this marriage united the Jacksons from the paternal and maternal lines of our father's genealogy.

Andrew and Miranda were both born in Salisbury, Connecticut. A story that is told as part of the oral history is that one of the Jacksons was a Native American and was raised by a white man. Was this Andrew or was it another Jackson? In any event, this part of our genealogy remains a mystery. Andrew, it is said, would go off into the woods alone for days at a time and live close to nature. He loved to whittle and often created toys for his boys. He was a hard working farmer and day laborer. His four big, strapping sons, Irving, Lewis, Andrew and Charles, were a joy to Andrew and his wife, Ida. In those days, one needed all the hands one could get to farm the land and make a living. The little girl that Ida so wanted died as an infant. Interestingly Andrew and Ida also migrated to Ansonia.

Since we have been researching our genealogy, we have met for the first time the offspring of Irving and the offspring of Lewis, two of our grandfather Charles's brothers. We are grateful to have had an opportunity to share memories, pictures and information with Allan Potter, grandson of Irving Jackson and Lewis Jackson, grandson of Lewis. The third brother, Andrew, had no children. We learned that each summer in the 1900s the Jacksons would get together for family celebrations and to visit one another. They often gathered in Pine Plains, New York where part of the Jackson clan settled. We as children did not go to these gatherings. Our side of the family, due to the divorce of our grandparents, had become estranged from the Jacksons. This was a missed opportunity.

The marriage of Agnes Adeline and Charles produced nine children. One of whom was Blyden Jackson, our father. He was born in Ansonia in 1905. Two years later Agnes Adeline and Charles and their family moved to New Haven, Connecticut. Early on, she became active in the life of St. Luke's Episcopal Church. She taught Sunday School, assisted with the choir, and worked with the Girls' Friendly Organization, a group that ran activities for young girls in the church. She was the right hand of the minister and a pillar of the church. The stability of the black family was very much evident in the families that attended St. Luke's. The minister, Father John H. Edwards, was revered by his congregation. He christened our father, Blyden in 1909, and much later christened the authors when they were a year old.

Agnes Adeline was very stern and like her mother, Miranda, she did not take much foolishness. Each of her children learned to cook. While one or two stayed home to cook the meal on Sundays, the rest of the family went to church. The children sang in the choir, were acolytes, and helped with Sunday School. Blyden, our Father, was also a Boy Scout leader. Agnes Adeline and Charles eventually divorced and times were difficult for the family. Blyden dropped out of school early to work. He did odd jobs and eventually drove a van for a moving company for many years.

In 1935, Blyden married our mother, Gertrude Lohman from Meriden, Connecticut. They had three children, Blyden Jr., Adeline and Alene. The latter two are the authors. Gertrude already had three children, from a previous marriage to a Mr.

Raymond Clayton. Raymond Jr., James and Jane Clayton are our step brothers and sister. Our father traveled across this country in his truck earning a living. He always sent us a post card picturing the places where he traveled. We were taught the work ethic by our parents who labored to provide for our family and give us a loving home. Our father was good in math and each of us would line up with our homework to get help. We often felt that had he been given the opportunity, he might have furthered his education.

The life of the Jackson family is a thread that weaves through the fabric of Connecticut's history. The Jacksons were present from earliest times and contributed to the growth of this state. They lived, loved and labored in Connecticut. We feel a spiritual connection to this land.

Chapter Three

The Fowlers of Dutchess County, New York

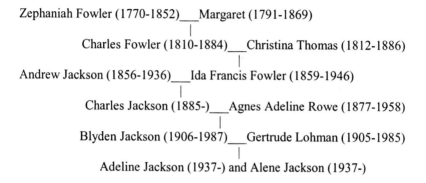

Zephaniah Fowler (1770-1852)___Margaret (1791-1869)

Charles Fowler (1810-1884)___Christina Thomas (1812-1886)

Andrew Jackson (1856-1936)___Ida Francis Fowler (1859-1946)

Charles Jackson (1885-)___Agnes Adeline Rowe (1877-1958)

Blyden Jackson (1906-1987)___Gertrude Lohman (1905-1985)

Adeline Jackson (1937-) and Alene Jackson (1937-)

For many generations our ancestors traversed the old Indian trails, that later became major roadways, between north west Litchfield and north east Dutchess Counties. They lived and married not only in the towns in Litchfield County but in the area called Nine Corners in Dutchess County which is a series of small farming towns nestled in the Berkshire Mountains: Amenia, Pine Plains, Milan, Washington, Stanford, Clinton, Northeast, Pleasant Valley, and Hyde Park. We read in Van Alystyne (1983)[1] the names of our relatives who are buried in the Smithfield Cemetery in north east Amenia. Thus our pilgrimage took us to Dutchess County.

One sunny afternoon in 1996, we journeyed to Smithfield. We drove through the mountainous area down around a winding road past some cows contentedly grazing in the field. We came upon a small white church and just across the road sitting near an old red barn was a small, lovely old cemetery with very old headstones. Some of them could not be read because they were weather worn. As we approached the head stones, we could imagine a scene of folks walking over the mountain range following a horse drawn cart carrying someone to his or her resting place. Upon entering the cemetery, off in the distance we could see the rolling hills with farmhouses nestled in between. What a beautiful pastoral setting. We proceeded to walk up and down the aisles of head stones and came across one with the Fowler name on it. We started yelling, "Here's one, here's one." Directly in front of us were the head stones of our 3rd Gt Grandparents Zephaniah Fowler (1770-1852) and Margaret Fowler (1791-1869); and our 2nd Gt Grandparents Charles G. Fowler (1810-1884) and Christina Thomas Fowler (1812-1886); all in a row in one place. What elation! What a spiritual moment! We felt like we were standing on sacred ground. Also buried in the Fowler row was Benjamin Fowler (1757-1843). We have not been able to establish his relationship to the others. Is he our 4th Gt Grandfather or the brother of Zephaniah? We have traced the Fowlers back six generations in Dutchess County.

One of the things we noticed when visiting the cemetery was the number of young children of Charles and Christina who were buried there: a daughter, Frances Mary, died in 1837 at age 1; a son, Austin G., died in 1839 at age 8; a son, Benjamin H., died in 1841 at age 1, and in that same year a daughter, Charlotte Jane, died at 1 month; a son, Charles, died in 1848 at 2 years; and lastly a daughter, Mary E., died in 1864 at 8 years. Since no reason was given for the deaths, we could not help but wonder how many were affected by the epidemics of cholera in 1832-1854 and the smallpox epidemic in 1862, and what the health care was like for them. It was in 1850 that the Board of Health was formed in Dutchess County. The Fowlers, as well as many other families suffered mightily during this period. Noteworthy, and still to be pursued, is the fact that Benjamin H. who died at age 1 year had the same name as the person buried in the row of Fowlers who was 86 when he died.

The headstones of the Fowlers were large and prominent and formed a family plot. This seemed to say something about their status in the community. They must have had some money in order to afford these headstones. As we stood there, we could only wonder what they looked like, what they endured, and what life was like for them in the early centuries of this nation, particularly as an African American Family.

The Fowlers lived in Dutchess County as far back as the 1700s. They are listed in the census as Free Blacks.[2] We believe they made their living by farming. In 1995, the Dutchess County Historical Society did a survey of the Smithfield Community of the 1860s. Interestingly, the "Smithfield Valley Project Survey"[3] identifies our 2nd Gt Grandparents, Charles and Christina Fowler, as living north of the Presbyterian Church in the house they rented. This was the church we had seen as we drove to the cemetery. The location was near the Smithfield Cemetery. Charles is identified as a butcher with $300.00 worth of possessions. He and his wife Christina had seven children ages 1 ½ to 27 years old. The three oldest children worked as laborers or domestics on local farms. There were three unrelated people living with them. During this period of time, it was not unusual for farm households to take others into their homes. You might find a large family with boarders who were laborers and domestics as in the case of the Fowlers. Even the physician, Dr. Isaac Hunting, who lived across the street from the Fowlers, took in the local clergyman, an Irish domestic and a farmer and his wife. Approximately ten thousand families lived on the farms in Dutchess County.

In the area, they grew wheat, hay, potatoes, apples, corn, oats, rye and barley. Sheep, swine, horses, cows, oxen and calves were raised on this land. There were also milk factories, and the best known was Gail Borden's Farm. Borden was known for having supplied the Union Army with condensed milk during the Civil War. Charles, Benjamin and Augustus Fowler fought in the Civil War. They were from Dutchess County and we believe they were part of our extended family.

Oral history tells the story that Charles Fowler helped to found the Smithfield Church. One gets the sense that the Fowlers were very much a part of the Smithfield Community. As a butcher, Charles must have had many opportunities to converse with his neighbors about the goings on in that community. Christina was a homemaker, and she spent her days raising seven children, cooking, sewing, canning and baking. One of Charles and Christina's daughters was Ida; she is our Great Grandmother. Later she married Andrew Jackson from Salisbury, Connecticut.

From the union of Andrew and Ida would come four sons: Irving, Lewis, Andrew and Charles, our Grandfather. It was Irving, born in 1896 in Pine Plains, who grew up and remained there. As an adult, he worked for many years at the Knickerbocker Farm (later known as the Osofsky Farm). He and his family were tenant farmers. The farm became the site of numerous family celebrations and gatherings. The Poughkeepsie Journal published a book about the Hudson Valley Region. The life of the Fowlers is chronicled and a picture of Andrew and Ida along with their four sons is shown.[4] The article indicates the longevity of the Fowlers and Jacksons as freed African Americans in Dutchess County dating back to the early 1700s.

Blyden Jackson (Father)
Alene, Adeline, & Blyden Jackson

The Authors
Adeline Jackson Tucker & Alene Jackson Smith

Father
Blyden Brown Jackson
1906-1987

Mother
Gertrude Lohman Jackson
1905-1985

Uncle George Jackson / Grandma Jackson / Father Jackson
George Jr. / Jane Clayton / Jimmy Clayton / Twins
Blyden Jr.

Paternal Gt. Gt. Grandfather
Richard S. (Koonk a Pot) Jackson
1817-1896

Paternal Gt. Grandmother
Miranda Jackson Rowe
1855-1947

Paternal Grandmother
Agnes Adeline Rowe Jackson
1877-1958

Gt. Grandfather George Clinton Rowe, 1853-1903 Gt. Grandmother Miranda Jackson Rowe, 1855-1947	Unknown Gt. Gt. Grandmother Adeline Agnes Starr F. Rowe, 1827-1899

Benedict   *Litchfield*

Paternal Gt. Gt. Grandmother
Adeline Agnes Starr F. Rowe
1827-1899

Children of George Rowe and Miranda Jackson Rowe

| Blyden
Rowe | Bessie
Rowe
Parquer | Agnes
Adeline
Rowe
Jackson | Clarisa
Deming
Rowe
Blue | Wilamena
George
Rowe
Carter |

Paternal Gt. Grandparents
Andrew James Jackson
1856-1936
Ida Frances Fowler Jackson
1859-1946

Sons:
Lewis, Irving, Andrew, and
Charles (our Grandfather, 1885)

Harriette Fowler
1861-1944
Ida Fowler's sister

Smithfield Church
in Amenia, N. Y.

Smithfield Cemetery, Amenia, N. Y.
Family Plot

Chapter Four

The Rowes of Litchfield, Connecticut

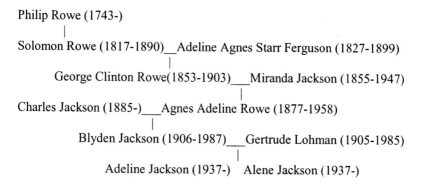

Philip Rowe (1743-)

Solomon Rowe (1817-1890)___Adeline Agnes Starr Ferguson (1827-1899)

George Clinton Rowe(1853-1903)___Miranda Jackson (1855-1947)

Charles Jackson (1885-)___Agnes Adeline Rowe (1877-1958)

Blyden Jackson (1906-1987)___Gertrude Lohman (1905-1985)

Adeline Jackson (1937-)   Alene Jackson (1937-)

We return to Litchfield County to tell the story of the Rowes. This northern family gives us another glimpse of what life was like for the northern African American in early America. One of the Rowes, a son of the north, will eventually leave New England and go South. It is his journey that will fill the remaining pages of this saga.

We knew our family had its roots in the town of Litchfield but we did not know the extent. While researching the Rowes, another branch of our family, we came across an interesting passage in a local history book by Gold (1904).[1]

History of Cornwall.

"Old Sol, oldest son of old Phil Rowe, with whom I played in my boyhood, went to Litchfield, and enjoyed respect in that aristocratic town for his personal character and dignified appearance. Another descendant of Phil became a useful minister in the South. Old Phil amused the boys in reciting stories of suffering in slavery but generally they received kind treatment and in return rendered faithful service."

We were utterly surprised and taken aback when we read this. The quote both delighted and sobered us. It delighted us because it gave us information about three generations of Rowes and it sobered us because this was the first hint we had that one of our relatives had been a slave in Connecticut. The Rowe's roots can be traced back to Philip Rowe, our 3rd great-grandfather and the first generation of Rowes. From what we can gather he was born in the late 1700s as a slave in Goshen, Connecticut which is part of Litchfield County. How long he was enslaved, who his master was and the circumstances of his manumission are undetermined. He gained his freedom sometime in the early 1800s. The Connecticut Census of 1830 shows Philip Rowe living in Goshen as a free Black.[2] He was between the ages of 24 and 36. He was married and had one daughter.

The second generation was Solomon, Phil's oldest son. We know, from records in the town hall of Goshen, that Solomon had a brother named Samuel. Solomon was born in Goshen in 1817. We no not know what life was like for him as a young man. However, we do know that he married a woman from Goshen, Connecticut named Adeline Agnes Starr Ferguson, our second great-grandmother. Solomon and Adeline were married in St. Michael's Church in Litchfield on January 13, 1841. The announcement of their marriage appeared in The Mercury Newspaper on January 21, 1841.[3] The Rowes then settled in Litchfield. They were one of only a few African American families in that town. They were treated respectfully and were involved in the life of the community.

Arthur Bostwick in the Alain C. White book (1920),[4] states the following:

> "In my boyhood, Litchfield had lately been a purely American community, by which I mean one inhabited almost solely by families of English descent. There were only half a dozen negroes or so, and the Irish had only recently begun to come in. ...The negroes were not employed as house servants or in general outdoor work about houses. They were not coachmen or

gardeners, but were manual laborers on outside jobs. In the South, black and white boys play freely together. What the southerner is particular about is not social contact, but social status. The latter did not worry us, but there were only two Negro boys, as I recollect, who associated with us. One was Charles Nicholas Doute, a West Indian, brought here as a servant by the McNeills. ...The other was Sam Rowe, the son of Solomon Rowe, sexton of St. Michael's Church. The Rowes were altogether a notable family. Their hospitality was without stint, and their little shack, already bursting with the Rowe family, was warranted to hold as many guests as applied for admission. Sol was a wit. When a certain young rector, who had business interests in New York, used to absent himself from his duties, so frequently as to cause remark, Sol said, "I can always tell when Mr. X is going to be away, for the Sunday before he always preaches from the text: 'It is expedient that I should leave you.'

The Rowes, I believe, had been Northern for some generations."

This passage sets the Rowe family in a social context that gives information about their life-style and life in general at that time, particularly for Blacks. This passage also indicates that some Africans came as servants of White families as well as slaves. Interestingly enough, Solomon Rowe became sexton of St. Michael's Episcopal church where he served for fifteen years, from 1865-1880. He would "rise early to stoke the fires, ring the bell, sweep and dust." Brewster (1954)[5] also mentions Solomon. It seems that Solomon was quite a wit and a man of good humor. He often told amusing stories which made a lasting impression on the community of Litchfield. The book further states that the Rector of St. Michaels, at that time, The Reverend Dr. Storrs Ozias Seymour, often told anecdotes about Solomon Rowe because Rowe was apparently his own man. Dr. Seymour said he felt as though he should include in the announcements of a service, "God and Solomon willing."

When Solomon retired as sexton, The Reverend Seymour paid a tribute to him. His retirement statement appeared in the town paper, The Litchfield Enquirer, on May 20, 1880. It read that he retired "with pleasant memories of, and many thanks for, your kindness to me and my family during my service."[6] We do not know much about Solomon's wife Adeline Agnes Starr Ferguson. We do know that the Rowes were a close knit, hospitable family whose doors were always open to friends and family. Picnicking at Bantam Lake was probably a favorite pastime for the Rowes. It appears that Solomon and Adeline were very supportive of their children and provided many opportunities for them. The Rowes eventually purchased a home on North Lake Street in Litchfield in 1864 and later built an addition onto it to house their growing family.[7] Discovering these passages in local history books was like unearthing an archeological treasure that put a personality to the Rowe family. These ancestors no longer were just names, but were now real people.

Life had its hardships and its joys. As was common in those days, the Rowes lost a son and three daughters in childhood. Cemetery records[8] indicate that Caroline died in 1847 at age 2, Elizabeth died in 1848 at age 1, and Sara died at 18 months in 1850. One can only surmise that they died of those diseases that afflicted so many children in the 1800s. A statement in The Litchfield Enquirer on Thursday, November 3, 1859 states that on October 25, 1859 Gilbert Rowe, oldest son of Solomon and Adeline, died in Goshen, Connecticut.[9] He died of typhoid fever at age 12.

By 1860, we would surmise that the joy of the Rowes' lives were their three sons - Lewis age 11, Samuel, probably named after his father's brother, age 6 and George age 7, our Great Grandfather, and the George mentioned in the passage quoted about Old Phil and Old Sol. The boys were the third generation of Rowes dwelling in Litchfield. George Clinton Rowe, born May 1, 1853, would go on to become a pastor, a poet and an editor of a newspaper. With the benefit of education, George's generation of Rowes went on to greater accomplishments. They were second generation freedmen. The Rowe Boys received a common school education. Town records indicate that Lewis was married on July 8, 1874.[10] Samuel was musically inclined and in adulthood he directed a band and later organized a drum and bugle corp.[11]

Based on a photograph in later life, George grew to be a tall, lean, rather gentle boy, dark complexioned, with piercing eyes. He was a studious, pensive child who loved words. He often wandered in the hills of Litchfield gathering nature specimens and writing. Although he began writing poetry early in life, none of his early poems exist today. Words both written and spoken fascinated young George. He was eight years old when the Civil War broke out in April of 1861. There must have been much talk about slavery and the war in the Rowe household. The family probably followed events closely in their local newspaper, The Litchfield Enquirer. George, more than likely, heard the great orators of the day, such as Wendell Phillips, Frederick Douglass and others. Many of them were itinerant speakers who came to Litchfield to preach about temperance or the abolition of slavery. A notice in The Litchfield Enquirer on Thursday, January, 1873[12] tells of a gathering to be held in Washington, Connecticut, a small town a little distance from Litchfield, at the Congregational Church there. The speaker was to be Wendell Phillips, the great Abolitionist. By this time the railroad had come to Litchfield and one could pay fifty-five cents to take the Shepang Valley Railroad to the meeting. Perhaps George, who would later write a poem dedicated to Wendell Phillips, traveled to hear him speak. George was also greatly influenced by the Rev. Allan McLean, a great preacher and the minister at the First Congregational Church in Litchfield from 1875-1882. The Rowes were members of this church.

This Congregational Church and Litchfield itself was where Lyman Beecher, the great fiery orator preached from 1810 - 1826. Initially Beecher had slaves but in time gave them up. The Beechers left a legacy of abolitionism in Litchfield. Indeed

41

Beecher's daughter, Harriet Beecher Stowe, who was born in Litchfield would go on to write the famous novel, *Uncle Tom's Cabin*.

On January 20, 1870, an advertisement appeared in The Litchfield Enquirer:[13]

> WANTED. - A smart, energetic boy, about 15 years of age, To learn the Printing business. One residing in the village preferred. Apply immediately at this office.

It could be assumed that George answered this ad because at the age of 17 he became an apprentice at The Litchfield Enquirer, the leading local paper. The proprietor at that time was George A. Hickox. After three years, George received a certificate of trade in Litchfield, Connecticut, the first "colored" man to do this. The certificate was granted when a person had worked to learn all aspects of the printing trade. This was truly an excellent outlet for George to express his ideas and use his writing skills. Thus began a love affair with the printed word.

As a newspaperman, he had an interest in social, political and economic events. He was aware of the aftermath of the Civil War, the Reconstruction in the South, and the plight of the Negro in America. He realized there were poverty and wretched conditions, lack of education for the freedmen and generally very few opportunities. He was deeply troubled by what he read and heard but he was also optimistic about the future of African Americans.

George wanted desperately to serve his people. He felt one way was to study Theology. His intent at that time was not to be a minister but to study the Bible and use this background for educational purposes. Thus he began to study under the tutelage of a mentor. The Rev. Allan McLean may have been instrumental in this process. Many years later George would dedicate one of his poems to the Rev. McLean.[14] After several years, George was examined by the Board of Examiners of Yale

College, in Litchfield. The Board was a group of Congregational Ministers who asked a candidate questions related to his studies and if he passed, he was recommended for ordination as a minister. Although George passed the examination, he did not feel he was quite ready to be ordained. He chose not to become a minister at that time. George was a man of varied talents and interests. Not only was he a newspaperman, an avid writer of poetry, and student of Theology, three strands that would be interwoven throughout his life, he also had an abiding interest in Natural History. He collected rocks, birds' eggs and reptiles. He later donated his large collection to various schools in Litchfield. The education of young people was always a concern of his. He felt young people could benefit from such a collection.

It was the early 1870s and George had met a young woman, Miranda Jackson, our Great Grandmother, from Salisbury, Connecticut. Miranda's parents, Richard and Mary, were farmers in Salisbury. On July 8, 1874, George, who was 21, and Miranda, who was 19, were married in Litchfield.[15] Shortly thereafter they began their family and had two children in Litchfield - George Jr., born April 1875, and Agnes Adeline, born February 22, 1877. Agnes Adeline is our grandmother.[16]

What began as a small voice in George's heart and head crescendoed into a deep longing to go South and work among his people. He wanted to use his skills and knowledge as he stated, "to elevate the race" and particularly the young people. George was aware of the work that the Church and others were doing in the South to help the ex-slaves. The First Congregational Church in Litchfield sent personnel and monies to help such institutions as Hampton Institute in Virginia and Avery Institute in South Carolina to thrive. In fact, Harriet Richards, the daughter of a former Congregational Minister in Litchfield, was the head of the "Indian Department" at Hampton Institute and her sister was a teacher. It may have been because of Litchfield's connection with Hampton that George became aware of the fact that Hampton needed someone to run its

Printing Department. George saw this as an opportunity to use his skills as a printer and also to work with his people.

Miranda knew that George longed to go South. Many hours were spent discussing the pros and cons of this move. It would be a big decision for the Rowes. They had never ventured far from home before, and they had a young family to think about. However, George made a decision that would determine the rest of his life. In 1877, he and his young family moved South, leaving their beloved New England.

Chapter Five

A Northern Son's Sojourn South: Hampton Virginia

Twelve years after the end of the Civil War, in June 1877, George Clinton Rowe, at the age of twenty-four, left Connecticut and went south to Virginia with his family to live. Born and raised in the North, this Connecticut Yankee would go south with zeal to work among his people. This was the fulfillment of a long held dream. George found an opportunity to use the skills he had learned as an apprentice at The Litchfield Enquirer. He secured a job as head of the Printing Department of Hampton Institute. He immersed himself in his work at Hampton where he oversaw the publication of such journals as the American Missionary, the Southern Workman, and the Alumni Journal. The Southern Workman was devoted to the industrial classes of the South. It contained news and information related to both the Negro and the American Indian. At the time George was at Hampton, Native Americans were students there as well as African Americans.

George was greatly influenced by the American Missionary Journal. Having grown up in the Congregational Church in Connecticut, he was aware of the role the American Missionary Association was playing in establishing churches and schools in the South. The Congregational Church was instrumental in the formation of the AMA in 1846. This organization was a Christian Missionary Society dedicated to spreading the gospel of Christ. It was opposed to slavery, and its mission was to help the Freedmen in the South. After the Civil War, the freed slaves were in dire straits. Most were not equipped to face freedom because they lacked the necessary skills such as reading and writing. The AMA played a large role in addressing these needs by selecting northern teachers and preachers to go to the South as "Missionaries" to teach and preach.[1] We believe this is where the notion that Rowe was a missionary to Africa came about. Over time, the fact that he was a so called "Missionary" to the South became a story that he was a missionary to Africa.

In all our research, we have nothing to indicate that this was the case.

The American Missionary Association established the first day-school among the Freedmen on September 17, 1861 in Virginia. That school laid the foundation for the Hampton Institute and was the forerunner of hundreds of schools sponsored by the AMA for the purpose of educating African Americans.

In one of the editions of the <u>Southern Workman</u> in 1881, there appeared an advertisement in the classified section indicating that George Rowe was a dealer in stationery, fancy goods, and picture frames.[2] This surely could provide much needed income for a young struggling family. George and Miranda had two additional sons while they were at Hampton. They named the boys Phillip and Blyden. Phillip was the name of George's Grandfather, who had been a slave. Blyden was the name of Dr. Edward W. Blyden, Founder and President of Liberia College in Africa. Dr. Blyden was a frequent visitor, to Hampton, and he gave his inaugural address to the student body at Hampton on January 1881. He must have had a strong influence on George. In that same edition of the 1881 <u>Southern Workman</u>, there appeared a letter from Booker T. Washington. He had been a student at Hampton and graduated just before George arrived. The letter tells of his accomplishments and aspirations for Tuskegee Institute.

The seeds of George Rowe's ministry were nurtured while he was at Hampton. One Sunday morning, several children were playing outside his home. He approached them and struck up a conversation. Instead of George going to the local church, he decided to ask the children in and they sang and prayed with his family. A Sunday morning ritual grew from three children to 350 as time passed. Needless to say the gathering grew too large for the Rowe home, and a friend at Hampton allowed them to use the Ocean Cottage on Hampton's Campus. Thus began the Ocean Cottage Church School under the auspices of George Clinton Rowe. He was always concerned with educating youth and giving them a Christian upbringing. His wife, Miranda, also taught Sunday School. This became an excellent opportunity for George to develop his ministerial skills. The Ocean Cottage Sunday School, built by Hampton Normal and Agricultural Institute students about 1879, was the forerunner of the Little England Chapel. This Chapel was built with funds given by Daniel F. Coch, a White man. Today it is on the Historic Registry and is the only known Black missionary chapel in the Commonwealth of Virginia.[3]

Interestingly enough in one of the editions of the <u>Southern Workman</u> in 1879, George tells of the formation of this Church School.[4] He goes on to say that the First Congregational Church in Litchfield, his home church, sent 350 Sunday School books for him to use with his new Sunday School. George continued his association with his home church in Connecticut, thus maintaining a spiritual lifeline with the church that nurtured him as a boy.

George witnessed an historic event while he was at Hampton, the burning of Academic Hall, one of the buildings on campus, on November 8, 1879. Years later he would write a poem about the "structure grand and noble."[5] He recalled the good work that took place in that building and how it had helped a struggling race. The building was used for classrooms, offices, and living space. It also housed, temporarily, a boys' dormitory and the printing office.

The Rowes had to make many adjustments in their new life in the South. Prior to that time they had not met with the depth of prejudice and segregation exhibited in Virginia. This had to have saddened George who felt strongly about the worth and dignity of all men. These were very stressful times for the Rowes. Miranda had four young children. George was trying to establish his career, study, work at the press and run a small enterprise on the side. There were times when they longed for home and the New England they fondly remembered. However, they were both committed to and hopeful about the future of the race. George's religious convictions spurred him on, and his poetry became a therapeutic outlet for him. .

His connection with the AMA finally influenced him to make a vital decision. After six years at Hampton, he decided to be ordained. He used his remaining time at Hampton to reflect and prepare for his next move. He had much to do. He had to make arrangements to be ordained. He knew this would involve another move because he would be sent to an area where there was a great need. In 1883, he met with the Litchfield (Conn.) South Consociation and entered the active ministry. Hampton was the setting for the ordination and the Georgia South Consociation performed the ceremony. The future was a bit uncertain, but armed with his faith and his family at his side, Rowe took a position at a church in rural Georgia.

BURNING OF ACADEMIC HALL

The Sabbath, day of holy thought and rest,
Is ending; and the waters of the creek,
Calm and placid 'neath the setting sun,
Suggest the rest prepared for saints above.
The Day of God with duties manifold,
And searchings of His Holy Word for light,
Has been devoutly spent in work for Him –
Performing deeds well-pleasing in His sight.

The hymn of praise and meek devotion, has
Been sung in harmony by many a voice;
And raising up, in faith, of heart and soul,
Unto the God whose name is Love, has brought
Its own reward in rest and peace.
               And o'er
The gray old town of Hampton, picturesque
And sombre, with its wealth of memories
Historic and heroic, there now reigns
A dreamy silence and an hour of peace.

The sunset-tinted bosom of the bay
With boats and other crafts bestuded is,
Which gently sway and rock in restful mood,

48

Upon the sighing, swelling current.

                              List!
Soft on the air of eve, are borne sweet strains
Of music: 'tis the evening melody,
Which, day by day, comes sweetly stealing o'er
The intervening water from the Home: -
Retreat most beautiful, where now in peace,
Secure from battle din and strife of war,
There rest a thousand war-worn veterans.

Upon the breath of evening now we hear
The tones of bells—calling to prayer and praise
And worship—students of the Normal School;
Most fitting close of every earthly Sabbath –
An emblem, too, of the eternal Day
Of rest. That congregation vast arise
To sing the opening hymn in harmony
Which only they who in the rugged school
Of unrequited toil have served their day,
And felt the sweet relief—the pride and joy
Which perfect freedom gives—can sing; a strain
That thrills with joy the soul!

                        With rapid strides
A student enters; a mysterious look
Upon his countenance, as if possessed
Of knowledge of importance all unknown
Unto his fellows; and hastily imparts
That knowledge to his chief; and instantly
A hand is lifted and a silence reigns –
Full of suspense -- a silence
filled with dread!
Sure, in a moment so intense as this,
The mind, in seeming, lives for many years.
Then come the words which startle every one;
"Let girls remain, and men to duty pass—
On fire is Academic Hall!"

Now fierce and thrilling on the Sabbath peace

49

Rings out in fear the wild alarm bell!
The night is dark; and rushing figures, weird
In the lurid glare, appear like spectres—
Goblins grim and ghostly, on mischief bent,
Holding high carnival, with shout and dance,
In very truth a panorama grand!
A passing scene—bewildering, dazzling dream!

The engine whistle, shrill and piercing;
The fireman's shout; the startling spiteful hiss,
As stream in quick succession follows stream;
The crash of falling beams of giant size,
Bechill and curdle blood within the veins,
And cause throb with pain the beating heart.
Phantastic colors brightly blazing forth
From bursting chemicals add brilliancy
Unto a scene of dazzling awfulness.

The hungry flames in grim defiance of
The efforts made for their extinguishment
Leap high in pride and fury—laugh with scorn
At the exertions small and puny, which
Man with all his learning, art and wisdom,
Can now put forth, as grappling hand to hand
In battle stern with the dread Fire King,
He fights with all his might.

                              An hour is gone;
And in its train, the work of busy years.
A pensive sadness overhangs the scene;
For Academic Hall which yesternight,
The scene of joyous, active life had been,
Has vanished, and in place thereof, outlined
Against the southern sky, now towers
A skeleton, in hideous grimness.
That structure, grand and noble, is no more;
Yet, mem'ry of the work accomplished here
Within its walls, shall live for years to come,
In the unfolding power and manhood of
A struggling race!

Chapter Six

McIntosh, Georgia

As a newly ordained minister, George Rowe arrived from Virginia full of hope and expectations to McIntosh, Georgia in April 1883. He was to assume the duties of Pastor of the Cypress Slash Congregational Church. As Rowe traveled from the county seat to Cypress Slash, he noticed that the last five miles were only woods with an occasional log cabin set off the road among the trees. Upon arriving at the church, he noted how small but attractive the building was. It appeared small on the outside but once inside, the church was large enough to seat 300-400 people. It seemed strange that the church was so large for this rural community. Perhaps it had many uses, or they built anticipating the future. The parsonage next door was in pretty good shape but needed some repairs before Rowe could bring his ever-growing family there. It was a log cabin of two rooms, a two-story addition on one end and three large fireplaces. It was unfinished inside and needed work. Dense woods surrounded both the church and parsonage. In time, additional rooms were added and it made quite a comfortable home for the Rowes.

The church had seventy-five members. The first few times Rowe started the service on time even though many members were not there. He was an on-time man, and he wanted to establish that pattern early in his ministry. In time, his flock realized this, and they began to arrive on time. It did not take long for Rowe to gain a reputation as an outstanding preacher. He was sought after on the Georgia preaching circuit and other Southern locales. He spoke in the pulpits of many churches, at school graduations and at special ceremonies. His talks were uplifting and reflected his deep religious convictions. He immersed himself in the work of the Congregational Church in the South, becoming Statistical Secretary and the Treasurer for the Georgia Congregational Association. These duties involved many meetings and some travel to national meetings as well.

Rowe would both preach and teach in this rural area. In fact,

Rowe mentions in an article he wrote for the <u>Southern Workman</u> in September 1883, that he sat for the Exam for Teachers in Georgia.[1] He mentions that it was fourteen years since he left school. This seems to indicate that he might have taken some course work while he was at Hampton. George's work was cut out for him because the majority of the people were uneducated. He and his wife taught in the school. One of the first things he did was to start "The Palmetto" debating society among the youth. He always had high expectations for the young people. The young men were particularly bashful and awkward, giving rise to many humorous moments as they stuttered and stammered and flailed their arms to make their points. In time, they did quite well.[2]

Among other things, George gained a reputation as a fearless man. This was the result of an encounter he had with an alligator. In his travels to the homes of his congregation, he rounded a bend and an alligator stood hissing at him. George hit it once on the head and grabbed it by the tail and subdued it. The sexton at his church viewed this with disbelief, superstition and skepticism. The six foot tall sexton said, "Why Parson, I would not lay my hands on that thing for five buckets of gold."[3] Many were afraid of George because he was not afraid of alligators. George was a naturalist and his reputation grew as he collected alligators and reptiles for his collection; he skinned one alligator and stuffed it. He used his collection for educational purposes.

The South had enjoyed a period of progress during Reconstruction from about 1865 to the early 1870s, after which there began a reversal of the promising trends. Repressive laws began to be established to separate the races. Rowe could not accept the prejudice he encountered, however, and whenever he could, he fought against it, whether it was through the spoken or written word. He wrote articles for the <u>American Missionary Journal</u> and the <u>Southern Workman</u>. He expressed his feelings through his poetry. He preached against racism in his sermons, and he fought against it through organizational membership. He joined forces with other clergy in the South to rail against it.

Meanwhile, Rowe's family was growing. A daughter, Wilhelmina, was born. His ever-increasing family was a joy to him and his wife. The poetry he wrote was descriptive and the subject matter included events and things that touched his everyday life. Rowe had been in Georgia for four years when he was called to a church in Charleston, South Carolina. The following is a poem he wrote about Cypress Slash.[4]

CYPRESS SLASH

There's a place called Cypress Slash,
In the town of McIntosh;
'Tis a pleasant place to live,
And one's strength to missions give.
Many happy days we passed
In the bounds of Cypress Slash.

'Tis a farming district fine,
Where men and women spend their time
In the fields a-turning sod;
In sweet content they daily plod,
Clearing land of weeds and trash,
In the fields of Cypress Slash.

A mission church is standing there,
Siloam church, 'mid pines so fair;
On Sabbath, those who've six days trod
The fields, look up to Nature's God—
Turning their minds from care and crash
To temple praise in Cypress Slash.

Another church—the A. M. E.—
Stands near a grove of tall pine trees,
And there, on every Thursday night
The "Locals" preach with much delight,
And strike the book with mighty crash,
Down in the vale of Cypress Slash.

But with each month comes Brother G.—

A priest of common sense is he!
Oh, what a change comes o'er that band
Under his firm and steady hand!
Until he's gone, no noise, no clash,
In the valley church of Cypress Slash.

Of youth and maidens there's no lack,
And many of them on the track
That leads to brighter scenes above,
Where all is peace and joy and love.
But they are modest, shy, abash,
These boys and girls of Cypress Slash.

In the happy hours of spring
The woodland songsters sweetly sing;
Bees are humming in the bowers,
Where bloom the rose and jasmin flowers,
And at evening fire-flies flash,
O'er the fields of Cypress Slash.

Come, then, friends, and see the place,
And its rural populace;
In their simple, happy homes,
Where peace and joy and plenty comes,
We'll give you welcome, and some—"hash"
If you visit Cypress Slash.

Chapter Seven

Charleston, South Carolina

Charleston became a hub of activity for Blacks after the Civil War. They outnumbered the Whites and they lived in all sections of Charleston. Large concentrations of African Americans lived in Wards 2 and 4. By the late 1800s, they were moving in larger numbers to the upper wards of the city. A real class system became more pronounced among the African Americans. There was the upper class, made up of mainly Mulatto families. Many of these families felt they were of a higher station than those freed slaves who were uneducated and held menial jobs. This was the Charleston of Martin Delaney, a native of Pennsylvania who moved to Charleston. He was an abolitionist, a Union Army Officer and a graduate of Harvard who came to Charleston to practice medicine. This was elegant Charleston, a place where after the Civil War and during Reconstruction, Blacks began to take advantage of the few opportunities that were beginning to open to them. The Rev. Richard H. Cain was elected a state legislator in 1870. The Rollins Family was another prominent Charleston family. One of the daughters, Frances Rollins, would later become a Whipple, marrying William Whipple, a leading black lawyer in Charleston. She would also write the famous biography of Martin Delaney.[1]

Blacks were enjoying some advances in the South during the Reconstruction Period. However, by 1887 when Rowe arrived in Charleston, the racial climate was changing. The period of progress was waning. The resentment Whites felt toward Black gains started to really surface and laws began to be passed to reverse those gains. By 1889, South Carolina's Civil Rights Law was repealed. Legally enforced racial segregation came into existence.

It was this legacy that Rowe inherited when he arrived in Charleston to become pastor of the Plymouth Congregational Church, that was established in 1867. Blacks before this date had attended the Circular Congregational Church of Charleston which was mainly White. After the edifice was destroyed during the Great Fire of 1861, many Black congregants left Circular and started their own church. They met in an old chapel of Circular Church for awhile and then in 1867 established Plymouth Congregational Church. George Clinton Rowe was the tenth pastor of Plymouth. It was indeed an honor for him to accept this pastorate. It was his oratorical skills and leadership ability that brought him to the attention of those searching for a new minister. He was delighted to be there. Plymouth gave him a new pulpit from which to preach and lead. He moved his family to Charleston with high hopes and great ambitions.

Rowe played many roles as pastor of Plymouth and a leader in the community, foremost being his work at Avery Institute. Pastors at Plymouth were expected to spend some portion of their time at Avery, and Rowe was no exception. Avery Institute was one of the educational institutions started by the American Missionary Association after the Civil War. It was held in high regard by African Americans. Rowe spoke each year at Avery's Commencement and gave inspirational talks at assemblies. He continued his love of poetry. In spite of his heavy schedule, he authored several books of poetry that were used as part of the curriculum at Avery. His inspirational poems exalted African American heroes and heroines. Such figures as Robert Smalls, who commandeered the Planter, a Confederate Ship, during the Civil War in Charleston Harbor and Richard Cain, minister and politician who was elected to the South Carolina State House of Representatives during Reconstruction, were subjects of his poetry. These were men who influenced Rowe and whom he admired. Drago (1990)[2] describes the inspirational nature of the literature and history taught by the Yankee Missionaries. He mentions as an example one of George's books of poetry entitled *Our Heroes*.[3] In 1890, Avery celebrated its 25th Anniversary. The graduation that year was indeed a special occasion. George wrote a poem and dedicated it to Avery Institute.

Miranda, Rowe's wife, also participated in the life of Avery, assisting whenever she was needed. However, she still had a family to raise. The family now included seven children - George Jr. and Adeline born in Connecticut, Phillip and Blyden born in Virginia, Wilhelmina born in Georgia, and Miranda and Clarisa born in South Carolina. Some of the Rowe children attended Avery. We believe Adeline, our grandmother, attended. She later became a teacher. Wilhelmina also attended but we do not have a record of the others.

George had been an AMA minister for about ten years when he arrived at Plymouth Church. While he was grateful for all this organization had done for him as well as for his people, one of his goals was to make Plymouth self-sufficient. He wanted Plymouth to raise its own money and be able to pay its own expenses. It took a while, but he accomplished this under his pastorate. One of the other goals was to build a larger parsonage. This he also accomplished. The Rowes were able to move their large family into the new parsonage located on the corner of Pitt and Bull Streets in Charleston.

In 1886, a devastating earthquake hit Charleston. The city sustained quite a bit of damage. The death toll was great. Somehow Plymouth Church remained relatively untouched. Rowe was part of a group of Black Clergy who were in the forefront of the rescue efforts, doing all they could to help bring relief to their people who suffered mightily from this disaster.[4]

Rowe was president of the Charleston Ministerial Association. As such, he befriended many of the Southern Leaders of that time not only in Charleston but in Georgia and North Carolina as well. He wrote a memorial to the Rev. Joseph C. Price, who was President of Livingstone College in Salisbury, North Carolina and who died in 1894 at the peak of his career.[5]

Black teachers had no real opportunity to teach in the Charleston public schools, not even those schools that had Black children. A committee of ministers led by George C. Rowe in March 1896 went from Charleston to Columbia, South Carolina to lobby for a bill which would change this practice. The lobby failed, but they struggled on. Rowe loathed the increasing violence toward Blacks in the South. He and other leaders from Charleston attended the anti-lynching convention held at Columbia, South Carolina in the late 1800s. Blacks were trying to mobilize their forces to demonstrate against the vicious attacks on their people. Rowe preached vehemently against this practice from his pulpit.

Once a newspaper man, always a newspaper man. George Rowe had started his career at The Litchfield Enquirer back in Connecticut. Now he had come full circle. He began a weekly newspaper aptly called the Charleston Enquirer, no doubt as a tribute to the Litchfield paper of the same name and where he received his initial training. Rowe's small shop was located on King Street in Charleston. He wrote of local events and Republican issues as well as articles related to the Temperance Movement. His paper served to inform the Blacks of Charleston of events in the world. Moore (1988),[6] notes the following: "The Charleston Enquirer was a weekly, prohibition, republican, Black publication established 1892 and ceased publication in 1901. George Clinton Rowe was editor and publisher." Two of Rowe's sons, Phillip and Blyden, assisted their father at the newspaper working on the presses. African American Newspapers served to educate the Black community.

George Clinton Rowe's philosophy can be summed up from one of his addresses delivered at Claflin University, Orangeburg, South Carolina on April 26, 1892. It was entitled "The Aim Of Life: Live, Learn, Labor, Love."[7] Indeed Rowe did this to the fullest. He lived a full and exemplary life. He died October 3, 1903 at the age of 50. His obituary appeared in the AMA Journal.[8]

Indeed Rowe was a great Renaissance man. He was a pastor, poet, editor, naturalist, educator and fighter for the rights of his people. He used all his talents to help make the world a better place. Although his life was cut short, his living was not in vain.

George Clinton Rowe born April 1853 in Litchfield, Connecticut traveled South to preach and teach among his people. He left his beloved New England imbued with the abolitionist spirit nurtured in Connecticut, and he led an exemplary life. He would never return to live in his beloved New England, but a poem he wrote many years earlier called "Retrospect" sums up his feelings.[9] See the poetry chapter.

In 1995, we had the opportunity to visit Charleston, South Carolina. We immediately went to Pitt and Bull Streets to see if Plymouth was still there. The old building remains and it is an institute for the deaf today. But the edifice looks like it did in Rowe's day. You can tell it was once a church. We went in and asked if we could look around. We could feel the spirits of our ancestors. Here is where our Great Grandfather did indeed live, learn, labor and love. Our eyes tried to soak up every inch of the place. It was a great spiritual moment for us. Of course today there is a new Plymouth Church in Charleston. The present minister, the Rev. Fields, was gracious in showing us around Charleston and giving us a bit of its history.

Yours ever,

Geo. C. Rowe.

Chapter Eight

The Poetry of George Clinton Rowe

I think of those days full of brightness,-
*   The fields and the meadows so green;*
The brook with its ripple of gladness,
*   Where minnows and trout could be seen...*
Of picnics enjoyed in the wildwood,
*   By the side of the "big" Bantam Lake[1]...,*

These poetic words from "retrospect" were penned by George Clinton Rowe, a naturalist whose love of nature is evident in his poetry. Litchfield, Connecticut was a particularly picturesque, serene location which lent itself to the long contemplative walks Rowe probably loved to take as a youngster. It provided a beautiful backdrop which surely inspired him to write his poetry. George Rowe moved from Litchfield to Hampton, Virginia in 1877 to work in the Printing Department at Hampton Institute. Although he was working and had a young family and was a busy man, he still found solace in his poetry. It was while he was at Hampton that he published his first pamphlet of poetry entitled "Sunbeams." Unfortunately this 1877 edition is long out of print.

Hampton Institute was one of the American Missionary Association sponsored schools that was started to help educate the numbers of freed Blacks after the Civil War. It was a beacon of hope for a race of people long held in bondage. It was here that Rowe began his spiritual service to his people by organizing a Sunday School.

One fateful night on November 9, 1879, Academic Hall, one of the main buildings on campus that housed classrooms, dormitory space, and the printing press office, caught fire and was destroyed. This horrendous event inspired George and he captured this historical moment in one of his poems entitled "Burning of Academic Hall." Surely, as Rowe says in the last verse,

...For Academic Hall which yesternight,
The scene of joyous, active life had been,
Has vanished, and in place thereof, outlined
Against the southern sky, now towers
A skeleton, in hideous grimness.
That structure, grand and noble, is no more;
Yet, mem'ry of the work accomplished here
Within its walls, shall live for years to come,
In the unfolding power and manhood of
A struggling race![2]

George Rowe spent five years in Virginia and then moved to Cypress Slash, Georgia where he was ordained and pastored a church for three years. In 1885, he moved to Charleston, South Carolina where he became the tenth pastor of Plymouth Congregational Church. There he published his first collection of poetry entitled *Thoughts In Verse.*[3] The poems in this collection chronicle his life's experiences and people who were dear to him. In the introduction to the collection, Rowe speaks about the fact that not many African Americans had written poetry. He hoped that his collection "may do something towards stirring up our young people to higher aspirations."[4] Part I is a dedication and he writes a poem in tribute to his mother, Adeline, for her love and devotion.

Part II is entitled Sunbeams and these poems express love and appreciation for a variety of people. Perhaps the sunbeams are those people who brought light and joy to his life. What connection these have to his original poem entitled Sunbeam is not clear. At least three of the poems in this section are written for his daughters - Agnes Adeline, our grandmother; Wilhelmina; and Mary.

Part III, entitled Memoriam, is dedicated to people who influenced his life. He writes of Wendell Phillips, a leading abolitionist during slavery, and The Rev. Allan McLean, a Congregational Minister from Litchfield, Connecticut who was a mentor to him. He then devotes Part IV to poems related to the

Psalms.

Part V is entitled Bethesda and contains a selection of poems about people and places. "Retrospect" and "Burning of Academic Hall" are in this section. His poetry has a decided religious overtone and is lyrical in quality. He uses poetic language to express his thoughts and feelings.

The poem entitled "Retrospect," which introduced the chapter, is particularly poignant and seems to capture the nostalgia George was feeling. One can just imagine George Clinton Rowe, a man of great perseverance and dedication to his work, allowing himself a moment of reflection and longing as he thought back to a time and place that was so dear to him. Yet these memories seem to have fortified him for the work he had to do. Although he visited on occasion to preach at the Congregational Church in Litchfield or for a family funeral, Rowe never returned to live in his beloved Connecticut.

Rowe had a second collection of poetry published in 1890 entitled *Our Heroes. Patriotic Poems on Men, Women, and Sayings of the Negro Race.*[5] He wrote about such outstanding African Americans as Robert Smalls, Crispus Attucks, Toussaint L'Overture, Frances Ellen Harper and Lucy C. Laney. The poems in this collection were ballad type poems that are long, lyrical and tell a story. They reflect a historical event and lift up the contributions that African Americans have made. One such poem was "General Smalls." He was a slave and a seaman on the Planter, a Confederate gunboat during the Civil War. He piloted the Planter from the Confederate side to the Union side with members of his family aboard. He later became a representative from South Carolina to the U.S. Congress.

History was an important subject at Avery and according to Drago (1990), "The inspirational nature of the literature and history taught by the Yankee missionaries can be seen in the poems by George C. Rowe, the Plymouth pastor..."[6] Rowe's poetry was used in the history curriculum at Avery.

Different ages may judge his poetry differently. Whatever the literary value, his poems are a genealogist's delight. They serve as a road map of places he had been and when he was there and people he had interacted with and admired. In the poem written to his daughter, Agnes Adeline, we see names and relationships in the family. Truly these poems have historical value as well. They preserve the history of a people and those names, places and events that are important.

Jackson, not related, (1989),[7] states that "George Clinton Rowe may well be thought of as the last in time of the black poets from New England who probably should be associated with the Age of the Abolitionists."

RETROSPECT

As shadows of twilight are falling,
            And hushed is the voice of the sea,—
The chirp of the blue-bird is calling
            His mate to the airy home tree;
When nature seems resting from labor,
            Then joyous, sweet memories come:
My mind wanders back to my childhood,
            I think of the loved ones at home.

I think of those days full of brightness,—
            The fields and the meadows so green;
The brook with its ripple of gladness,
            Where minnows and trout could be seen
Darting blithely from cover to cover
            Of the banks, where the lazy cows come
To drink 'ere the long day is over,
            And the cow-boy should hurry them home.

Of picnics enjoyed in the wildwood,
            By the side of the "Big" Bantam Lake;
The glad, happy voices of childhood
            Which ever such sweet music make.

I think of the rides on the hay-load,
            From the meadow down through the big gate,

The shrill, piping note of the tree-toad
          That warned us 'twas growing quite late.

I think of the nightingale singing
          In the apple-tree over the way,
At evening, with notes clear and ringing;
          And how he was frightened away
By Tabby, the solemn old mouser,
          Who always was ready to dine,
(Except when he caught sight of Towser,)
          On a bird be he ever so fine.

I think of the slow-footed turtle
          That lived by the brook in the vale,
Where delicate violets and myrtle,
          And arbutus their fragrance exhale.
How he clumsily fell in the water,
          As the feet of the school-boy approach,
Fright'ning the chub *and the* sucker,
          And startling the shy little roach.

I think of the hole of the ground hog,
          By the tree on the side of the hill,
And how it was watched by old "Spring-dog,"
          Who ever was ready to kill.
He never considered it sinful
          To take life of a poor fellow beast,
But always was ready and waiting,
          And did not repent in the least.

I think of the home of the wood-thrush.
          By the side of the Indian cave—
Old "Benvenough," *where the firebush,*
          Like a beacon its fiery leaves wave.
The shelter and haunt of the robin,
          The woopecker's nest in the tree,
The song of the cat-bird at evening—
          All life seemed so happy and free!

I think of the hills and the mountains,
          Where many glad hours have been passed

65

In hunting, and reading, and thinking,
     And watching the dark clouds, that cast
A gloom over beautiful nature,
     Oft filling our bosoms with dread;
The thunder that pealed forth in grandeur
     The gleam of the lightning so red.

And then, too, I think of the sunset,
     As seen from the old Prospect Hill,
How he gradually sunk in the far West,
     With his light other countries to fill.
And thoughts that are brought by the sunset
     And fleece-clouds by gentle winds driven;
Oh! the glory and beauty resplendent!
     It seemed like a vision of Heaven!

I think of those days without shadow,
     Each one was a separate gem;
Those walks to the brook in the meadow,
     Conversing with dear Cousin Em.
Who long since has gone from earth's shadow,
     To the land where the weary may rest,—
No fear of the coming to-morrow
     Disturbs the repose of the blest.

I think of the faces of playmates,
     Which long ago vanished away
From earth, now with many a loved one,
     In the land of continual day.
Of teachers who taught on the Sabbath
     The truths which by Jesus were given,—
To come, thou must suffer the children,
     For of such is the Kingdom of Heaven.

I think of the rides on the railroad,
     The slow-going, winding Shepang,
Running down through the hills and valleys,
     The snow, and the rain and the fog,—
To hear the great speeches of Phillips,
     Of Boudinot, Holland and Gough,—
Which filled us with longings for greatness,

In the science of letters and thought.

And, as my mind wanders this evening,
 To the far-away scenes of the past—
The hopes and the fears and repinings,
 And pleasures too intense to last,
My heart is cast down, full of sadness,
 As I think of the hours yet to come,
Or trial, and struggle,—once gladness,—
 So changed from the old days at home.

The bright days of childhood have vanished,
 And with them, full many a dream,
Of wealth, and of greatness have perished—
 This old world is not what it seems.
And, as I arouse from my rev'rie,
 Confronting the cares which have come,
With manhood's full day to perplex me,—
 I long for the old days at home.

PART I.

DEDICATION

This volume is affectionately dedicated to my Mother, Mrs. Adeline S. Rowe.

MOTHER.

Pure is the love that we give to thee, mother,
 The purest and sweetest by mortals possessed;
A love that we cannot allow to another,
 And there is no love in this cold world more blest.

In infancy, childhood and youth, thou did'st guide us;

67

When Christian instruction most freely was given—
'Twas thy loving teaching that pointed to Jesus,
    To Jesus, to life, to a bright home in Heaven.

And were we bereft of thy presence, dear mother,
    The half of life's sunshine would flee from our heart:
For friendship, or father, or sister or brother,
    Could not fill thy place, if from thee we must part.

And for the great love thou hast given so freely,
    We'll cherish thee, love thee, until the last breath,
And we will, God helping us, shield thee from evil,
    And cheer thy dear heart till the shadow of death

Is o'er thee, and then, in the mansions of glory,
    We'll think of thee happy with angels of love;
And when we have finished the work Christ has given
    Us
    We'll meet thee, and greet thee, in Heaven above.

AGNES

To Agnes Adeline Rowe:

There is a winning little girl,
With dark brown eyes, and auburn curl,—
The name of this—my little pearl—
    Is Agnes.

She is a cheerful little thing,
Happy as robins on the wing—
Which in the summer sweetly sing—
    My Agnes.

To-day, she is just five years old—
Washington's birth-day, too, I'm told;
And she is dearer far than gold.
    My Agnes.

Be kind to all you chance to meet;
Run errands of love with willing feet;
That grateful friends may ever greet
  Thee, Agnes.

Love grandpa, grandma, mamma, too,
And Uncle Sam—they all love you,
To George, Phil, Blyden, e'er be true,—
  My Agnes.

Learn all you can where'er you go,
Of nature's secrets,—where wild flowers grow,
And with Aunt Millie learn to row.
  My Agnes.

May God in kindness look on thee,
And many birthday's may you see.
And may you ever happy be—
  My Agnes.

May all your life be pure and bright.
Illumined o'er with virtue's light,
And happy as it is to-night—
  Dear Agnes.

Feb. 22d, 1882.

EIGHTEEN

To Mary:

 Our life is like a river,
   Ne'er ceasing in its flow,—
It rushes on forever,—
   The swift years come and go,
Bearing us on their current,
   To happiness or woe.

May yours be spent in wisdom,
    In profitable employ;
May deepest peace and freedom,
    And happiness and joy
Flow on with you, my sister,
    And trouble ne'er annoy.

And when the domes and mansions
    Immortal may be seen,
When but the River Jordan,
    So peaceful intervenes,
May we be just as hopeful
    As when you were eighteen!

WILHELMINA

I know a maid of gentle grace,
    With eyes like stars of night,
With such a lovely, beaming face,—
    Where'er she is 'tis light!

I have a secret—shall I tell,
    That every one may know?
I love this little maiden well—
    Sweet Wilhelmina Rowe.

She has a large place in my heart,
    'Tis hers where'er I go.
May we as lovers never part—
    Sweet Wilhelmina Rowe.

And may Our Father's loving care
    Protect from every foe;
A benediction is my prayer,—
    For Wilhelmina Rowe.

GENERAL SMALLS

It was in Charleston Harbor,
Nigh thirty years ago,
That the gallant steamer Planter
With grace plied to and fro,
Ladened with ammunition
And food for Boys in Gray,
Within the forts, that for defence,
Surrounding Charleston lay.

There was among the sailors
A Negro, good and true,
Who much preferred to Southern gray
A uniform of blue.
He worked within the wheel-house;
He knew the signal calls
And he resolved to run the lines—
His name was Robert Smalls.

Before the other sailors
He doth his plan unfold,
And all but two think liberty
Dearer than life or gold.
And so they make arrangements:
"No matter what befalls,
We'll make a run for freedom!"
Said the heroic Smalls.

The ship lies at its moorings
Near the "City by the Sea,"
The officers to spend the night
And with companions be,
Have left the ship well ladened
With guns and cannon balls,
Four sailors true, the engineer
And pilot, Robert Smalls.

The night was dark and lonely,
The hour was three o'clock;
When quietly the Planter

71

Was steamed up to the dock.
Aboard their wives and children
In haste the leader calls;
It is an hour with danger fraught
For hero, Robert Smalls!

Now, out upon the Harbor
He steers with steady hand;
The shores look dark, forbidding,
As he gazes to the land.
The reach the point, Fort Sumter,
Attention! signal calls;
Promptly he blows the whistle
'Tis all right! Pilot Smalls.

He steams past Morris Island,
The signal answers back;
But Sumter signals "Something wrong!
Arrest her in her track!"
The guns from Morris Island,
With ready cannon balls,
Send forth a shower of iron hail
At Pilot Robert Smalls.

But he is out of danger!
'Tis an heroic feat!
With all his power he urges
Out to the Union fleet!
But they mistake his signal —
A storm of heavy balls
Are ready now to deal out death!
To gallant Robert Smalls!

Oh, joy! they see his signal,
And not a whit too soon!
To save a tragedy that night
Under the rising moon!
But 'twas a happy moment
As e'er to moartal falls!
When the Union fleet received that ship

From hero, Robert Smalls!

They've reached the Port of Freedom.
    This gallant little band!
They sought the ground enchanted —
    To them earth's promised land!
For they had felt for many years,
    Grim slavery's crushing power!
It is a time supreme and blest —
    It is a triumph hour!

Detailed blockading pilot
    He served the cause with pluck!
A guide to the Crusader,
    The Stono, — Keokuk.
He made repeated trips along
    The river, near the shore,
Removing the torpedoes thence
    Which he had sunk before.

Sailing through Folly Island creek,
    Under Confederate gun,
The Planter *then was in command*
    Of Captain Nickerson, —
Commander was demoralized
    As the leaden shower falls,
Fearless he takes the Captain's place —
    Promoted! Captain Smalls!

He served the Union 'till the end
    Of the great civil strife;
Then, as a leader of his race,
    He entered public life.
With honor served his native State
    As Representative.
His work within the Senate will
    For generations live!

And in the State militia
    He filled an honored place,
First Colonel, then a Brigadier,

73

He served with skill and grace;
Then Major-General of the troops —
This title to him falls.
These places with distinction
Are filled by General Smalls.

At National Convention,
In eighteen-seventy-two
He votes for Grant and Wilson,
Those noble men, and true!
In seventy-six and eighty
He's called upon again,
To stand by Hayes and Wheeler;
For Logan and for Blaine.

And then he served in Congress,
With faithfulness, six years:
A sturdy man, of common-sense,
Consistent, without fears!
We feel in him peculiar pride,
As his record to us falls;
For he has acted well his part —
Honest *Congressman Smalls.*

He failed of re-election
But not from failing vote;
Because the honest (?) Democrats
Counted our hero out.
But he is not defeated —
To him our ruler calls!
The message: You're appointed
Collector, Robert Smalls.

In canvassing for General Smalls
A good Republican
Said — "I believe in all the world
Smalls is the greatest man!"
"Who's greater?" "Why, the Lord, of course,
His match was never met!"
"Ah!" he replied, triumphantly;
"Smalls is a young man yet!"

74

(Postscript)

He stood before the altar,
        And, standing by his side,
A noble woman, good and true,
        A loving, trusting bride.
He trembled *when he said "I will;"*
        And perspiration falls, —
This man of war, and Congress,
        Our hero, General Smalls.

"I knew the General, 'fore the war
        For fifteen years or more;
I'm sure that he was never known
        To tremble so before!"
Well, many a man can calmly face
        Musket and cannon balls,
Who fears to face a lady fair, —
        No wonder! General Smalls!

They gather in his lovely home,
        At Beaufort's ocean side,
His friends and guests, to wish him joy,
        And see his winning bride.
We wish thee all the blessing
        That mortal lot befalls,
Prosperity, and length of days —
        General, and Mrs. Smalls!

NOTES
Introduction
1. William D. Piersen, *Black Yankees* (Amherst: The University of Massachusetts Press, 1988), Appendix, Table 1.
2. Lorenzo J. Greene, *The Negro in Colonial New England* (New York: Atheneum, 1969), Appendix, E345.
3. Benjamin Quarles, *The Negro in the Making of America* (New York: Simon & Schuster,1987), Foreword 17.

Chapter One
1. Connecticut Federal Census, 1790.
2. Rev. G.F. Goodenough, Ed. *Ellsworth, Connecticut* (Amenia, NY: Times Press, 1890), 59.
3. Military Records. Federal Pension Records from the Revolutionary War, National Archives, Washington, D.C.
4. Danbury Land Records, Book 2, 132, June 11, 1783.
5. National Society Daughters of the American Revolution, *Minority Military Service Connecticut 1775-1783* (Washington, D.C.: 1988).
6. David O. White, *Connecticut's Black Soldiers 1775-1783,* A Publication of the American Revolution Bicentennial Commission of Connecticut (Chester, Conn.: Pequot Press, 1973).
7. See note 3.
8. Probate Court Records from Sharon, Connecticut. Land Deeds 1818-1827 for Robert and Lilly Starr. Vol. 18 & 19, p. 434, 4331 # 1391-92.
9. Hartford County Court Records, 1833.
10. Lawrence VanAlstyne, *Born, Married and Died in Sharon, Connecticut* (Sharon, Connecticut: Press of Pawling Chronicle, 1897), 120.
11. See note 2.

12. Edward C. Starr, *A History of Cornwall, Connecticut* (New Haven, Conn.: Tuttle More House Taylor Co., 1926), 210 and 414.

13. Records from the Calhoun Cemetery in Cornwall, Connecticut.

14. Probate Court District of Sharon, Connecticut. Last Will and Testament of Abel C. Starr. March 28, 1881, Recorded Probate book 27, 18.

15. Rev. Henry G. Marshall, late Captain of Company I Twenty-Ninth Connecticut Volunteers, "History of the Twenty-Ninth (Colored) Regiment C.V. Infantry," *Record of Connecticut Men in the War of the Rebellion 1861-1865* (Hartford, Conn: Adjutants - General, 1889).

16. J.J. Hill, *A Sketch of the 29th Regiment of Connecticut Colored Troops: Story of the Battles of the 29th* (Baltimore, Maryland: Daugherty Maguire & Co., 1867).

Chapter Two

1. Constance Baker Motley, *Equal Justice Under Law* (New York: Farrar, Straus and Giroux, 1998), 25.

2. Theodore S. Gold, *Historical Records of the Town of Cornwall, Litchfield County Connecticut,* 2nd ed. (Hartford, Conn: The Case, Lockwood and Brainard Co., 1904), 361-362.

3. Francis Atwater, *History of Kent, Connecticut* (Meriden, Conn: The Journal Pub. Co. 1897).

4. Connecticut Federal Census for 1830 and 1840.

5. Connecticut Federal Census for 1850.

6. Bureau of Vital Statistics, State of Connecticut, Town of Ansonia, Certificate of Death Richard Jackson, March 23, 1896.

7. See note 4

8. See note 5

9. Connecticut Federal Census for 1860.

10. Connecticut Federal Census for 1870.

11. Town of Litchfield, Connecticut, Vital Statistics,

Record of Marriages 1874, Vol. 35, pages 328-329.

12. Town of Litchfield, Connecticut, Vital Statistics, Record of Marriages 1876, Vol. 35.

13. Bureau of Records and Statistics, Department of Health City of New York. Certificate of Death Miranda Jackson, April 15, 1947.

Chapter Three

1. Lawrence VanAlystyne, *"Smithfield Burying Ground.,"* *Burying Grounds of Sharon, Connecticut, Amenia and North East, New York* (New York: Heart of the Lakes Publishing, 1983).

2. Alice Eichholz and James M. Rose, *Free Blacks Heads of Households in the New York State Federal Census, 1790-1830* (Detroit, Michigan: Book Tower, 1981).

3. The Smithfield Valley Project. A report to the Architecture, Planning and Design Program, New York State Council on the Arts. Prepared by Dutchess Land Conservancy, Stanfordville, New York, 1993.

4. Poughkeepsie Journal, *The Hudson Valley Our Heritage, Our Future* (Pub. in the U.S. by the Poughkeepsie Journal, 2000), 5 and 11.

Chapter Four

1. Theodore S. Gold, *Historical Records of the Town of Cornwall. Litchfield County Connecticut* 2nd Ed. (Hartford, Conn: The Case, Lockwood & Brainard Company, 1904), 368.

2. Connecticut Federal Census, 1830

3. The Mercury, January 21, 1841. Married in Litchfield by the Rev. Mr. Payne, (St. Michael's) January 13, 1841, Mr. Solomon Rowe to Miss Adeline S. Ferguson.

4. Arthur E. Bostwick, Chapter XXII in Alain C.

White, *The History of the Town of Litchfield,
Connecticut 1720-1920* (Litchfield, Conn.:
Enquirer Print, 1920), 233-234.

5. Mary B. Brewster, *St. Michael's Parish. Litchfield,
Connecticut 1745-1954* (Meriden, Conn: The
Journal Publishing Co., 1954).

6. Litchfield Enquirer, May 20, 1880.

7. Probate Records, Deed for Rowe Property, LLR
61:579. Old Koser House on North Lake Street
built in 1840. "Only documented 19th Century
residence of a Black family in Litchfield.

8. Charles Thomas Payne, (Transcriber). *Litchfield &
Morris Inscriptions* (Litchfield, Conn.: Published
by Dwight C. Kilbourn, 1906), 98.

9. See note 6, November 1859.

10. Town of Litchfield, Connecticut, Vital Statistics,
Vol. 35, page 328-329. Marriage of Lewis
Rowe and Anna St. John.

11 See note 6, November 11, 1897.

12 See note 6, January 23, 1873.

13. See note 6, January 20, 1870.

14. George Clinton Rowe, "Rev. Allan McLean,"
Thoughts In Verse (Charleston, South Carolina:
Kahrs, Stolze & Welch, Printers, 1887), 41

15. Town of Litchfield, Connecticut, Vital Statistics,
Marriage of George Clinton Rowe and Miranda
Jackson, July 8, 1874.

16. Town of Litchfield, Connecticut, Vital Statistics,
Birth of Agnes Adeline Rowe, February 22,
1877.

Chapter Five

1. A. Knighton Stanley, *The Children Is Crying.
Congregationalism Among Black People* (New
York: The Pilgrim Press,1979).

2. "Advertisement," Southern Workman, Hampton,
Virginia. April 1881, 48.

3. Pamphlet entitled: Little England Chapel. Hampton, Virginia.

4. George Clinton Rowe, "The Ocean Cottage Sunday School," <u>Southern Workman</u>, Hampton, Virginia, March 1879, 33.

5. George Clinton Rowe, "Burning of Academic Hall," *Thoughts In Verse* (Charleston, South Carolina: Kahrs, Stolze & Welch, Printers, 1887), 67-70

Chapter Six

1. George Clinton Rowe, <u>Southern Workman</u>, Hampton, Virginia, "Letter From Rev. Geo. C. Rowe," Cypress Slash, McIntosh, Liberty County, Georgia, September 1883, 94

2. See note 1, Hampton, Virginia, September 1883, 94.

3. See note 1, Hampton, Virginia, September 1883, 94.

4. George Clinton Rowe, *"Cypress Slash,"* *Thoughts In Verse* (Charleston, South Carolina: Kahrs, Stolze & Welch, Printers, 1887),33-34.

Chapter Seven

1. Bernard E. Powers, Jr., *Black Charlestonians. A Social History, 1822-1885* (Fayetteville, Arkansas: The University of Arkansas Press, 1994).

2. Edmund L. Drago, *Initiative, Paternalism, and Race Relations. Charleston's Avery Normal Institute* (London, England: The University of Georgia Press, 1990).

3. George Clinton Rowe, *Our Heroes. Patriotic Poems on Men, Women and Sayings of the Negro Race* (Charleston, South Carolina: Walker, Evans & Cogswell Co. 1890).

4. <u>The Cleveland Gazette</u>, September 18, 1886, Vol. No. 5, p. 1

5. George Clinton Rowe, <u>A Noble Life. Memorial Souvenir of Rev. Jos. C. Price, D.D.</u> (Charleston, South Carolina, 1894).

6. John Hammond Moore, Editor. <u>South Carolina Newspapers</u> (Columbia, South Carolina: University of South Carolina Press, 1988), 39.

7. Address by George Clinton Rowe entitled "The Aim of Life: Live, Learn, Labor, Love". Delivered at Claflin University Orangeburg, South Carolina on April 26, 1892.

8. *The American Missionary Fifty-Seventh Annual Report, "Obituary of The Rev. George C. Rowe, "* November 1903, 282.

9. George Clinton Rowe, "Retrospect" *Thoughts In Verse* (Charleston, South Carolina: Kahrs, Stolze & Welch, Printers, 1887), 63-67.

Chapter Eight

1. George Clinton Rowe, "Retrospect" *Thoughts In Verse* (Charleston, South Carolina: Kahrs, Stolze & Welch, Printers, 1887), 63-67.

2. See note 1, 67-69.

3. See note 1.

4. See note 1, Preface.

5. George Clinton Rowe, *Our Heroes. Patriotic Poems on Men, Women and Sayings of the Negro Race* (Charleston, South Carolina: Walker, Evans & CogswellCo., Printers, 1890).

6. Edmund L. Drago, *Initiatives, Paternalism, and Race Relations. Charleston's Avery Normal Institute* (London, England: The University of Georgia Press, 1990).

7. Blyden Jackson, *A History of Afro-American Literature. Vol I. The Long Beginning, 1746-1895* (Louisiana: Louisiana State Univ. Press, 1989).

Bibliography

Atwater, Francis. *History of Kent, Connecticut.* Meriden, Conn.: The Journal Pub. Co., 1897.

Brewster, Mary B. *St. Michael's Parish, Litchfield, Connecticut 1745-1954.* Meriden, Conn.: The Journal Publishing Co., 1954

Drago, Edmund L. *Initiative, Paternalism, and Race Relations. Charleston's Avery Normal Institute.* London, England: The University of Georgia Press, 1990.

Eichholz, Alice and James M. Rose. *Free Blacks Heads of House holds in the New York State Federal Census, 1790-1830.* Detroit, Michigan: Book Tower, 1981.

Gold, Theodore S. *Historical Records of the Town of Cornwall, Litchfield County Connecticut,* 2nd ed. Hartford, Conn.: The Case, Lockwood & Brainard Company, 1904.

Goodenough, Rev. G.F. Ed. *Ellsworth, Connecticut.* Amenia, New York: Times Press, 1890.

Greene, Lorenzo J. *The Negro in Colonial New England.* New York, New York: Atheneum, 1969.

Hill, J.J. *A Sketch of the 29th Regiment of Connecticut Colored Troops: Story of the Battles of the 29th.* Baltimore, Maryland: Daugherty Maguire &Co., 1867

Jackson, Blyden. *A History of Afro-American Literature. Vol I. The long Beginning 1746-1895.* Louisiana: Louisiana State Univ. Press, 1989.

Larson, Neil, Consultant. *The Smithfield Valley Project.* Stanfordville, New York: Prepared by Dutchess Land Conservancy, 1992.

Marshall, Henry G., Rev. *Record of Connecticut Men in the War of the Rebellion 1861-1865.* Hartford, Conn.: Adjutants-General, 1889.

Moore, John Hammond, Editor. *South Carolina Newspapers.* Columbia, South Carolina: University of South Carolina Press, 1988.

Motley, Constance Baker. *Equal Justice Under Law.* New York: Farrar, Straus and Giroux, 1998.

National Society Daughters of the American Revolution.
Minority Military Service Connecticut 1775-1783.
Washington, D.C., 1988.

Payne, Charles Thomas, Transcriber. *Litchfield & Morris Inscriptions.* Litchfield, Conn.: Published by Dwight C. Kilbourn, 1906.

Piersen, William D. *Black Yankees.* Amherst, Mass: The University of Massachusetts Press, 1988.

Poughkeepsie Journal. *The Hudson Valley Our Heritage, Our Future.* U.S.: Poughkeepsie Journal, 2000.

Powers, Bernard E., Jr. *Black Charlestonians. A Social History, 1822-1885.* Fayetteville, Arkansas: The University of Arkansas Press, 1994.

Quarles, Benjamin. *The Negro in the Making of America.* New York, New York: Simon & Schuster, 1987.

Rowe, George Clinton. *Our Heroes. Patriotic Poems on Men, Women and Sayings of the Negro Race.* Charleston, South Carolina: Walker, Evans & Cogswell Co., 1890.

Rowe, George Clinton. *Thoughts In Verse.* Charleston, South Carolina: Kahrs, Stolze & Welch,Printers, 1887.

Stanley, A. Knighton. *The Children is Crying. Congregationalism Among Black People.* New York, New York: The Pilgrim Press, 1979.

Starr, Edward C. *A History of Cornwall, Connecticut.* New Haven, Conn.: Tuttle More House Taylor Co., 1926

VanAlstyne, Lawrence. *Born, Married and Died in Sharon, Connecticut.* Sharon, Conn., Press of Pawling Chronicle, 1897.

VanAlstyne, Lawrence. *Burying Grounds of Sharon, Connecticut, Amenia and North East, New York.* New York: Heart of the Lakes Publishing, 1983.

White, Alain. *The History of the Town of Litchfield, Connecticut 1720-1920.* Litchfield, Connecticut: Enquirer Print, 1920.

White, David O. *Connecticut's Black Soldiers 1775-1783.* Chester, Conn.: Pequot Press, 1973.

Articles

"Obituary of the Rev. George Clinton Rowe." <u>The American Missionary</u> (November 1903): 282.

"The Ocean Cottage Sunday School," <u>Southern Workman</u> (March 1879) 33.

"Advertisement," <u>Southern Workman</u> (April 1881): 48.

"Letter From Rev. Geo. C. Rowe," <u>Southern Workman</u> (September 1883): 94.

George Clinton Rowe, <u>Southern Workman</u> (September 1883): 94.

George Clinton Rowe, <u>Southern Workman</u> (September 1883): 94.

Newspapers

The Cleveland Gazette (Ohio)

Litchfield Enquirer (Connecticut)

The Mercury (Connecticut)

About the Authors

Alene and Adeline are twin sisters who where born and raised in New Haven, Connecticut. They have traced their ancestors back six generations in Litchfield County, Connecticut, and Dutchess County, New York. The sisters have presented their research on both local and national levels. Alene Jackson Smith is an Associate Professor in the School of Education at Hunter College in New York City. She holds a doctorate from Columbia University Teachers College. Adeline Jackson Tucker is a Research Associate at the Yale Medical School.